Benchslapped:

Publicly Humiliating Judicial Opinions

Benchslapped:

Publicly Humiliating Judicial Opinions

Written and Edited by Matthew A. Bowers

Published by:
Travelers Series Publishing, LLC
11858 Bernardo Plaza Court
Suite 230
San Diego, CA 92128

ISBN-13: 978-1475144512
ISBN-10: 1475144512
BISAC: Law / Legal Profession

Dedicated to Annette Parker Bowers.
Without your support, I wouldn't be a lawyer.

Contents

Forward and Acknowledgments

I could claim a noble purpose for researching, writing and editing *Benchslapped*, but I'd be lying. The truth is that creating this book was a guilty pleasure. I expect reading it will be a guilty pleasure, too. I do not promise educational value, clever insights or continuing legal education credits. And though I made an effort to write readable prose and provide accurate citations, I make no guarantees regarding either. Nonetheless, I believe *Benchslapped* contains a number of witty legal opinions that are both enjoyable and educational.

A benchslap is salacious, but I'm drawn to more than the scandal surrounding a judicial takedown. What intrigues me is the narrative of each benchslap and the bizarre circumstances leading to it. As a result, this book is more than a compilation of legal snippets. It contains substantial passages drawn from the most interesting and amusing benchslaps ever published, with commentary and analysis throughout. These opinions address a broad range of malfeasance, including frivolous litigation, misconduct, rules violations, poor work product and insulting the bench. Although all readers may find this book entertaining, it is primarily a work for people who delight in (or simply can't look away from) a legal beat down.

I wish I could take all the credit for *Benchslapped*, but the real kudos belong to jurists across the country who are underpaid, overworked and forced to deal with the most contentious and unreasonable professionals on the planet. It is no wonder these civic heroes sometimes have to lay the smack down.

I must also recognize the bloggers and journalists who have worked hard in recent years to maximize attorneys' shame by sharing their benchslaps with the masses. Many of these bloggers are cited in this book. I give particular credit to Mr. David Lat, the creator and editor of the legal blogs Underneath Their Robes and Above The Law, who popularized (and perhaps invented) the term "benchslapped." Without his and other bloggers' tireless efforts, some of the greatest benchslaps of the modern era would go unnoticed and unappreciated, and my work to compile those benchslaps would have been significantly more difficult.

My business partner, Travis Medley, inspired me to take a simple idea and make it reality, and my good friend Jonathan Schwarzberg played an essential role in reviewing this manuscript and providing much-needed encouragement. Kristina Fredericks and Cynthia Tollett shared their big law experience and made extensive comments on early drafts. *Benchslapped* would never have been published without their advice and encouragement.

Finally, and most of all, I thank my patient wife and family, who encourage my hobbies, tolerate my eccentricities and slap me around only when I most deserve it.

CHAPTER 1: A Brief History of Benchslaps

The term "benchslap" has a short and ignominious history. It is derived from the misogynistic verb "to bitch-slap," which originated in the early 1990s. "Bitch-slap" is recognized by the Oxford English Dictionary, where it is defined as "to deliver a stinging slap to (a person), esp. in order to humiliate one regarded as inferior, *e.g., I would have bitch-slapped him for talking that way*."[1] The etymologists at OED, eager to avoid any improper usage, helpfully add that the term refers to "a woman hitting or haranguing her male partner," rather than to the subject of the slap. This distinction may be lost on the many would-be pimps and *machismos* who incorrectly use "bitch-slap" to mean "slap a bitch," resulting in a delightful irony: a group of the most deplorable chauvinists who call themselves "bitches" rather than describe their abuse.

Because "*bitch*-slap" refers to the origin of the slap, it follows that a "*bench*slap" refers to a slap delivered from the judicial bench. The slap is metaphorical, of course, and most often delivered through written opinions and transcripts. But many jurists would likely relish an opportunity to step down from the bench to issue some firm backhands. In fact, some judges, most notably Judge Ian Richards of the Broward County bench, have waded into the well to subdue violent or unruly litigants.[2] Other judges, including Ohio Municipal Court Judge Stephen Belden, Idaho State Court Judge Peter McDermott and Los Angeles Superior Court Judge Evertt Discksey, have had bailiffs duct tape parties' mouths shut.[3] These literal benchslaps must await fuller treatment in another book.

Baltimore personal injury lawyer John Bratt defines a benchslap as any "judicial opinion [that] makes it clear, in no uncertain terms, that a party has done something that was not appreciated."[4] This author prefers the broader and more colorful definition provided by the Urban Dictionary: "A benchslap is when a judge humiliates an attorney, insults another judge, or reverses a lower court in a particularly demeaning manner."[5] Attorneys may soon have more authoritative guidance regarding the term. Legal writing expert Bryan Garner, editor of *Black's Law Dictionary*, recently tweeted his interest in including "benchslap" in the next edition of that venerable reference book.[6]

Benchslaps are common. Most litigators worth their shingles have advanced aggressive or creative arguments and have been smacked down for it. Though humbling, these benchslaps are a necessary risk to protect clients' legal interests. This book is concerned with an entirely different kind of benchslap: where a judge, aside from addressing legal merits, uses a public opinion to criticize an attorney's intellect, character, ability or judgment. Some critiques question whether an attorney should even be allowed to practice law. As examples in this book demonstrate, benchslaps can be career-ending.

The term "benchslapped" was popularized in the mid-2000s by David Lat, the influential creator and editor of judicial gossip site Underneath Their Robes. Its usage was embraced and expanded by the legal blogosphere (the "blawgosphere") to the extent that it is common today throughout the legal industry, even by such distinguished legal superstars as Eugene Volokh, Alex Kozinski and Charles Nesson.[7]

Although any individual, party, attorney or judge can be benchslapped, this volume focuses only on judicial takedowns of legal counsel who appear to have demonstrated an exceptional lapse in skill, decorum or common sense. The word "lapse" is more appropriate than "lack" because, over the long and winding road of any legal career, even the most accomplished attorney or scholar can be bloodied by a judge's pen. Laugh at the humiliating benchslaps described in this book, but laugh nervously.

You could be next.

If blog postings, Internet comments and chain e-mails are any indication, attorneys are endlessly amused to see colleagues publicly dressed down by the Bench. Part of this is rubbernecking. Like all people, attorneys exhibit morbid curiosity when confronted by tragedy. One hopes there is more to it than pure *schadenfreude*, but attorneys can't help cringing when they read a benchslapping judicial opinion. Reputations are being tarnished. Clients are being lost. Career prospects are being crushed. Just as the highway motorist feels a sense of relief when passing a grave accident, a thorough benchslapping gives other attorneys an opportunity to reflect on their own good fortune at not being on the receiving end of a judicial smack down.

Of course, this may be giving the Bar too much credit. Perhaps attorneys just like to watch losers. Witnessing a spectacular failure can make people feel better about themselves, and even more so when it is a peer's failure. After all, *they* never would have made those comments, those choices or mistakes. Many attorneys believe wholeheartedly in their own infallibility until the very day they get benchslapped. At that moment, recoiling from their sudden infamy, they bemoan the unfairness of the judge who slapped them and the blawgosphere that made their shame public. And just as they once subtly mocked other victims of judicial smack downs, they begin receiving copies of humiliating opinions or transcripts in their inboxes from friends and colleagues, accompanied by words of consolation. Perhaps attorneys relish a benchslap because in the dog-eat-dog world of litigation each judicial takedown simply weakens the competition.

The good news is that the sting of even the most severe benchslap fades with time. Some attorneys even learn to laugh at the experience. And despite the sadistic enjoyment attorneys receive from reading about judicial takedowns, this author likes to think benchslaps provide learning opportunities. If nothing else, this compilation of benchslaps should give attorneys confidence that whatever mistakes they have made or will make in the future, someone has made that same mistake before them – and made it worse.

CHAPTER 2: Lawyers Behaving Badly

Licensed attorneys have no excuse for bad behavior. Nonetheless, it's common for a lawyer to cross the line of propriety in the name of zealous advocacy. Despite admonitions in model codes of conduct, including California's "Attorney Guidelines of Civility and Professionalism," many attorneys bicker like children caught breaking their mother's china.[8] Like good parents, judges have no choice but to haul these lawyers up by the ears until they behave.

Verbal chastisement for attorney squabbling is common in open court, but judges rarely include these reprimands in published opinions. It is profoundly embarrassing when a benchslap is published, even if it isn't career-ending. Consider the following benchslap, which was issued in response to a motion *in limine*. It opens with a procedural rebuke but quickly adopts a paternal tone:

The motions *in limine* were done incorrectly. Instead of a motion followed by a statement in support of it, the motion and the statement are mixed together, with the result that it is unclear what exactly the movant wants included or excluded; in plaintiffs' motion 1 for example, the substance of the motion is not stated until the conclusion of the argument section. . .

I again remind the parties to avoid tendentious bickering. Chamberlain's response is ridiculously argumentative, as in: "At bottom, Lear's motion is just another attempt to hide its willfulness and tip the case in its favor. Whereas Plaintiffs have been working with this Court in good faith to narrow the case in a fair and balanced way, Lear uses the concept of 'narrowing' as a sword and a shield. Just as Lear improperly invoked the attorney client privilege during discovery to hide its willfulness, Lear now latches onto the Court's desire to narrow this case to try to further hide its willfulness (while insisting all along that it should be allowed to use any helpful evidence it produced to show it acted carefully). Lear's actions are akin to a robber trying to hide years of evidence showing how he planned a robbery under the veiled argument that it is better for the jury to only hear about what happened the day the house was robbed, while at the same time introducing self-serving and irrelevant evidence from the prior period."

There must be no more of this childish abuse ("akin to a robber," etc.). Lear is at fault too but the plaintiffs are even worse offenders. No more or there will be sanctions. In more than 29 years as a judge, I have never encountered such bickering,

> "I have never encountered such bickering, quarrelsome lawyers. You are wasting my time and your clients' money…"

quarrelsome lawyers. You are wasting my time and your clients' money... [9]

Judge Richard Posner, Seventh Circuit

—————————————————

Judge Posner is not alone in his frustration over lawyers' apparent inability to get along. There is no shortage of written opinions comparing lawyers to babies and children. If anything, Judge Posner's benchslap is gentler than those leveled in the lower courts, where judges experience similar frustration even more acutely on account of discovery and law and motion practice. Judge Sam Sparks is the undisputed master of benchslaps (more on Judge Sparks in later chapters), and his witty sarcasm is on full display in the following takedown in the Southern District of Texas:

Be it remembered on the 1st day of July 2004 and the Court took time to make its daily review of the above-captioned case, and thereafter, enters the following:

When the undersigned accepted the appointment from the President of the United States of the position now held, he was ready to face the daily practice of law in federal courts with presumably competent lawyers. No one warned the undersigned that in many instances his responsibility would be the same as a person who supervised kindergarten.

Frankly, the undersigned would guess the lawyers in this case did not attend kindergarten as they never learned how to get along well with others. Notwithstanding the history of filings and antagonistic motions full of personal insults and requiring multiple discovery hearings, earning the disgust of this Court, the lawyers continue *ad infinitum.*

On July 20, 2004, the Court's schedule was interrupted by an emergency motion so the parties' deposition, which began on July 20, would and could proceed until 6:30 in the evening. No intelligent discussion of the issue was accomplished prior to the filing and service of the motion, even though the lawyers were in the same room. Over a telephone conference, the lawyers, of course, had inconsistent statements as to the support of their positions. On July 20, 2004, the Court entered an order allowing the plaintiffs/counter-defendants until July 23, 2004 two days from today to answer a counterclaim. Yet, on July 21, 2004, Bodyworx.com, Inc.'s lawyers filed a motion for reconsideration of that Court order arguing the pleadings should have been filed by July 19, 2004.

The Court simply wants to scream to these lawyers, "Get a life" or "Do you have any other cases?" or "When is the last time you registered for anger management classes?" Neither the world's problems nor this case will be determined by an answer to a counterclaim, which is four days late, even with the approval of the presiding judge.

> "The Court simply wants to scream at these lawyers, "Get a life…"

If the lawyers in this case do not change, immediately, their manner of practice and start conducting themselves as competent to practice in the federal court, the Court will contemplate and may enter an order requiring the parties to obtain new counsel.

In the event it is not clear from the above discussion, the Motion for Reconsideration is denied.[10]

Judge Sam Sparks, USDC, Southern District of Texas

Lawyer-on-lawyer conflict is a recurring problem for Judge Sparks. He was clearly driven to his breaking point by the attorneys in this next case, during which, via elegant couplets, he encourages counsel to face off against each other with six-shooters at noon and threatens them with incarceration "in a very cool cell." The opinion is reproduced here in its original form so as not to compromise the artistic integrity of Judge Sparks' use of white space.[11]

ORDER

BE IT REMEMBERED on the 25th day of April 2007 the Court reviewed the file in the above-styled cause, and specifically the defendant Hancock's Motion for Protection filed April 23, 2001, and after reading it a second time to make sure it was not a practical joke, the Court enters the following:

Stallions can drink water from a creek without a ripple;
The lawyers in this case must have a bottle with a nipple.

Babies learn to walk by scooting and falling;
These lawyers practice law by simply mauling

Each other and the judge, but this must end soon
(Maybe facing-off with six shooters at noon?)

Surely lawyers who practice in federal court can take
A deposition without a judge's order, for goodness sake.

First, the arguments about taking the deposition at all,
And now this—establishing their experience to be small.

So, let me tell you both and be abundantly clear:
If you can't work this without me, I will be near.

There will be a hearing with pablum to eat
And a very cool cell where you can meet

AND WORK OUT YOUR INFANTILE PROBLEM WITH THE DEPOSITION.

IT IS ORDERED that the Motion to Dismiss is DISMISSED.

SIGNED this the **25**th day of April 2007.

Sam Sparks

UNITED STATES DISTRICT JUDGE

An equally frustrated Judge Gregory Presnell issued the following opinion that, while less dramatic than guns at high noon, is more equitable:

This matter comes before the Court on Plaintiff's Motion to designate location of a Rule 30(b)(6) deposition (Doc. 105). Upon consideration of the Motion – the latest in a series of Gordian knots that the parties have been unable to untangle without enlisting the assistance of the federal courts – it is ORDERED that said Motion is DENIED. Instead, the Court will fashion a new form of alternative dispute resolution, to wit: at 4:00 P.M. on Friday, June 30, 2006, counsel shall convene at a neutral site agreeable to both parties. If counsel cannot agree on a neutral site, they shall meet on the front steps of the Sam M. Gibbons U.S. Courthouse, 801 North Florida Ave., Tampa, Florida 33602. Each lawyer shall be entitled to be accompanied by one paralegal who shall act as an attendant and witness. At that time and location, counsel shall engage in one (1) game of "rock, paper, scissors." The

> "At the time and location, counsel shall engage in one (1) game of 'rock, paper, scissors.' The winner of this engagement shall be entitled to select the location for [the deposition]…"

winner of this engagement shall be entitled to select the location for the 30(b)(6) deposition to be held somewhere in Hillsborough County during the period July 11-12, 2006. If either party disputes the outcome of this engagement, an appeal may be filed and a hearing will be held at 8:30 A.M. on Friday, July 7, 2006 before the undersigned in Courtroom 3, George C. Young United States Courthouse and Federal Building, 80 North Hughey Avenue, Orlando, Florida 32801.[12]

> Judge Gregory Presnell, USDC,
> Middle District of Florida

Although not career-ending, these benchslaps provide clear examples of how overzealous advocacy is often ineffective and even counterproductive. In 2010, there were nearly 300,000 civil cases pending in the 94 federal District Courts and another 77,000 criminal cases.[13] It is no wonder judges are impatient with lawyers who take the court's time to resolve minor disputes. In many instances, litigators' combative spirits render them incapable of recognizing how their behavior is perceived by neutral third parties. In the following opinion, Judge Eric Melgren is dumbfounded by an attorney's opposition brief to a trial continuance for the birth of opposing counsel's child. He issued the following public shaming in response:

"He who is his own lawyer has a fool for a client" is one of every lawyer's favorite proverbs. Among the several reasons why this is undoubtedly true, is that lawyers are trained to handle disputes skillfully but without the emotional rancor that will mask the actual parties' reason and good sense. Regrettably, many attorneys lose sight of their role as professionals, and personalize the dispute; converting the parties' disagreement into a lawyers' spat. This is unfortunate, and unprofessional, but sadly not uncommon. Before the Court, however, is an uncommon example of this unhappy trend.

This matter is currently set for trial commencing June 14, 2011. Defendants seek a brief continuance, noting that one of their counsel, Bryan Erman, along with his wife, is expecting their first child due on July 3. Given the proposed length of trial and the famous disregard that newborns (especially first-borns) have for such schedules, and given that the trial is scheduled in Kansas City while the new Erman's arrival is scheduled in Dallas, Defendants move this Court for a continuance. This in itself would not be remarkable, but in reviewing the motion the Court was more than somewhat surprised to read that "Plaintiffs have refused to agree to continue the trial setting and have indicated that they intend to oppose this Motion."

Well, every party is entitled to file an opposition to a motion, and hoping that perhaps Defendants' had mischaracterized the vigor of Plaintiffs' opposition, we have eagerly awaited Plaintiffs defense of its opposition. The Memorandum in Opposition arrived yesterday, and it was, sadly, as advertised.

First, Plaintiffs make a lengthy and spirited argument about when Defendants should have known this would happen, even citing a pretrial conference occurring in early November as a time when Mr. Erman "most certainly" would have known of the due date of his child, and even more astonishingly arguing that "utilizing simple math, the due date for Mr. Erman's child's birth would have been known on approximately Oct. 3, or shortly thereafter." For reasons of good taste which should be (though, apparently, are not) too obvious to explain, the Court declines to accept Plaintiffs' invitation to speculate on the time of conception of the Ermans' child.

Further, Plaintiffs assert that there are currently five attorneys from two different firms on Defendants' signature block. While the Court might be inclined to agree with Plaintiffs that this seems like a plethora of attorneys, it can't help but note that, entered and active on behalf of Plaintiffs in this case, are also five attorneys, from three different firms; so perhaps Plaintiffs are ill equipped to argue that Defendants have too many attorneys.

> "[This judge] has always tried not to confuse what he does with who he is, nor to distort the priorities of his day job with his life's role. Counsel are encouraged to order their priorities similarly."

Finally, Plaintiffs argue that surely Mr. Erman will have sufficient time to make it from the Kansas City trial to the Dallas birth, even helpfully pointing out the number of daily, non-stop flights between the two cities; and in any event complain of the inconvenience of this late requested continuance. Certainly this judge is convinced of the importance of federal court, but he has always tried not to confuse what he does with who he is, nor to distort the priorities of his day job with his life's role. Counsel are encouraged to order their priorities similarly.

Defendants' Motion is **GRANTED**.

The Ermans are **CONGRATULATED**.

IT IS SO ORDERED.[14]

> Judge Eric Melgren, USDC,
> District of Kansas

———————————

Judge Stephen Crocker of Wisconsin's Western District was similarly surprised by an opposing counsel's motion to strike a summary judgment motion that was electronically filed approximately four minutes late. He called out all nine attorneys by name in a hilarious and sarcastic benchslap of a denial.

Pursuant to the modified scheduling order, the parties in this case had until June 25, 2003 to file summary judgment motions. Any electronic document may be e-filed until midnight on the due date. In a scandalous affront to this court's deadlines, Microsoft did not file its summary judgment motion until 12:04:27 a.m. on June 26, 2003, with some supporting documents trickling in as late as 1:11:15 a.m. I don't know this personally because I was home sleeping, but that's what the court's computer docketing program says, so I'll accept it as true.

Microsoft's insouciance so flustered Hyperphrase that nine of its attorneys, namely Mark A. Cameli, Lynn M. Stathas,

> "Counsel used bold italics to make their point, a clear sign of grievous iniquity by one's foe."

Andrew W. Erlandson, Raymond P. Niro, Paul K. Vickrey, Raymond P. Niro, Jr., Robert Greenspoon, Matthew G. McAndrews, and William W. Flachsbart, promptly filed a motion to strike the summary judgment motion as untimely. Counsel used bolded italics to make their point, a clear sign of grievous iniquity by one's foe.

True, this court did enter an order on June 20, 2003 ordering the parties not to flyspeck each other, but how could such an order apply to a motion filed almost five minutes late? Microsoft's temerity was nothing short of a frontal assault on the precept of punctuality so cherished by and vital to this court. Wounded though this court may be by Microsoft's four minute and twenty-seven second dereliction of duty, it will transcend the affront and forgive the tardiness. Indeed, to demonstrate the even-handedness of its magnanimity, the court will allow Hyperphrase on some future occasion in this case to e-file a motion four minutes and thirty seconds late, with supporting documents to follow up to seventy-two minutes later. Having spent more than that amount of time on Hyperphrase's motion, it is now time to move on to the other Gordian problems confronting this court. Plaintiff's motion to strike is denied.[15]

Magistrate Judge Stephen Crocker, USDC,
Western District of Wisconsin

———————————————

Judges Melgren and Crocker are not the first to note the demise of the gentlemanly lawyer-statesman. Many have bemoaned the gradual ascendency of a breed of litigator that cannot draw the line between professional advocacy and personal rancor. However, the attorneys in the above cases likely had their clients' best interests at heart, even if their advocacy was overzealous and ultimately ineffective. Unfortunately, the same cannot be said for all misbehaving attorneys.

Take Hank Adorno, an attorney famous in the American Bar for all the wrong reasons. Mr. Adorno's legal star was once rising in South Florida. He had an enviable litigation track record and was co-founder of the nation's largest minority-owned law firm, Adorno & Yoss, which has more than 250 lawyers in 17 offices. In 2004, while purporting to act as class counsel for all Miami residents who paid a city fire service fee, Mr. Adorno negotiated a $7-million settlement that went to just seven of those residents. He received a $2-million dollar fee based on the settlement.

When Mr. Adorno's case came before Florida's Southern District and the Third Circuit Court of Appeals, they concluded he not only failed to advance his clients' interests but that he actually worked contrary to his clients' interests while representing them. The Third Circuit, in particular, would have none of it:

> It defies any bounds of ethical decency to view class
> counsel's actions as anything but a flagrant breach of fiduciary
> duty. . .

The evidence adduced at trial shows that the original plaintiffs misled the City's taxpayers into donating money for a class action that merely enriched seven individuals, who received a grossly disproportionate settlement amount. The amount the original plaintiffs settled upon bears no relation to the extent of any damages they paid in the form of assessments during prior years. The original plaintiffs admitted that they received a windfall from the settlement. The original plaintiffs, together with Adorno & Yoss, then conspired to keep silent about the settlement terms, to the detriment of the other taxpayers.

Adorno & Yoss' conduct further solidified the compromise of the class claims. The firm oversaw the settlement of $7 million which the parties agree could have otherwise resulted in a refund of $24 million to $70 million for the class. Additionally, Adorno & Yoss failed to move the class refund claims along, allowing the City to raise statute of limitations issues that were not otherwise available prior to the inequitable settlement. The language of the settlement actually called for a standstill of the litigation. Furthermore, at no time did Adorno & Yoss exercise candor before the trial court to explain the nature of the settlement. This reprehensible conduct alone is more than sufficient to establish a breach of fiduciary duty.[16]

Judge Juan Ramirez, Jr., Third Circuit

… Plainly and simply, this was a scheme to defraud. It was a case of unchecked avarice coupled with a total absence of shame on the part of the original lawyers. The attorneys manipulated the legal system for their own pecuniary gain and acted against their clients' interests by attempting to deprive them of monies to which they might otherwise be entitled. More unethical and reprehensible behavior by attorneys against their own clients is difficult to imagine.[17]

> "[This] was a case of unchecked avarice coupled with a total absence of shame on the part of the original lawyers."

Judge Angel Cortiñas, Third Circuit, concurring

The Third Circuit's benchslap was one of several Mr. Adorno received from both state and federal courts. He was eventually fined, disbarred and sued. Mr. Adorno's case proves a recurring proposition throughout this book: no one is immune to benchslaps. All lawyers, from the humblest solo practitioner to the department head of an AmLaw 100 firm, can be subject to the righteous castigation of the justice system. Some courts have gone so far as to benchslap an entire law firm in addition to individual attorneys practicing within the firm.

In 2008, a federal judge became so incensed by the antics of two highly regarded trial attorneys that he overturned a jury's $51 million verdict. On top of that, he ordered the offending lawyers to pay the fees and costs of opposing counsel – a sum totaling several million dollars. Senior Judge Richard P. Matsch sanctioned attorneys Terrance McMahon and Vera Elson of the prestigious international law firm McDermott, Will and Emery, as well as their entire law firm:

> Litigation misconduct is a basis for transferring the burden
> of attorney fees and expenses under both of the statutes relied

on by BrainLAB and the Court's inherent authority to supervise the conduct of litigation. In essence, the response from the plaintiff and MWE [Plaintiff's attorney's law firm], through new counsel, is that the Court had the obligation to stop any trial conduct that stepped over the line of zealous advocacy. In short, they argue that they should not be held responsible for what they were able to get away with during the trial presentation. The adamant denial that there was any abuse of advocacy in this case is in disregard of what this Court has already concluded and displays the same arrogance that has colored this case almost from its inception. Throughout these proceedings Medtronic and the MWE lawyers have demonstrated that when they are faced with adverse court rulings, they proceed undeterred, with only superficial observance of the court's determinations. . .

After the Court issued its claim construction rulings, Medtronic's counsel proceeded cavalierly, with reckless indifference to the merits of Medtronic's infringement claims. The continued prosecution of a claim after its lack of merit has become apparent warrants sanctions under § 1927. Shackelford, 96 F.Supp.2d at 1145. At trial, MWE's conduct was in disregard for the duty of candor, reflecting an attitude of "what can I get away with?" Throughout the trial, the MWE lawyers artfully avoided the limitations of the patent claims and created an illusion of infringement. They did so with full awareness that their case was without merit ...

> "MWE's conduct was in disregard for the duty of candor, reflecting an attitude of 'what can I get away with?'"

In this case, an award against the firm is appropriate. As the lead lawyers, Mr. McMahon and Ms. Elson were the most visible, but numerous MWE lawyers and support staff participated in the litigation and in the trial. Liability should be borne by the firm. If section 1927 does not support an award of fees against MWE as an entity, then such an award is appropriate under the court's inherent authority.[18]

> Judge Richard Matsch, USDC,
> District of Colorado[i]

One wishes the type of misconduct described in this last opinion was rare. It's easy to laugh at attorneys who fail to get along with one another or who, in a fit of adversarial pettiness, refuse to stipulate to a continuance. But these last examples of malfeasance involve attorneys whose overzealous advocacy jeopardizes justice in a more substantial way. Indeed, some attorneys see it as their legal duty to use civil procedure, discovery or an inherent weakness in the jury system to benefit their clients in any way possible, even if that use is improper. Like the attorneys described above, the threshold question for such attorneys may be "what can I get away with?," rather than "what is proper and ethical?"

---

[i] Like many of the judges profiled in this book, Judge Matsch has a reputation for running a tight ship. Larry Pozner, a Denver attorney and one-time vice president of the National Association of Criminal Defense Lawyers, once noted that, "In Denver, if you're going to be a federal trial lawyer, one stage is to be yelled at by Judge Matsch." Patrick E. Cole, *Don't Mess with Richard Matsch*, Time Magazine (May 26, 1997).

As a result of this increasingly prevalent approach to litigation, benchslaps involving serious judicial misconduct are easy to find. But because they are common, dry, seldom amusing and even depressing, they make few appearances in this book.

CHAPTER 3: Lessons Learned

Any conscientious attorney can learn from colleagues' benchslaps, but there are some judicial warnings that should provide guidance for even the most obtuse attorneys. For example, don't bicker with opposing counsel. Don't call them names in pleadings or accuse them of misconduct (absent extraordinary circumstances). And be reasonable. Reflect on how taking a combative stance on certain issues, like a trial continuance for the birth of a child, could be perceived by the court. Most importantly, before taking any action, ask whether it is ethical and in the client's best interests. Justice may be blind, but justices aren't stupid.

There are many paths to judicial admonition, and lawyers should learn lessons from those who have traveled those paths before. Taking a critical look at the benchslaps below can help attorneys devise a fairly simple blueprint to avoid similar punishment.

Just as good real estate agents rely on the mantra "location, location, location," so should any good attorney commit to the principle of "venue, venue, venue." Some judges are more prone to benchslaps than others. When presented with a choice, attorneys should steer clear of courts where benchslaps are delivered fast and loose, as they once were in the Texas courtroom of former U.S. District Court Judge Samuel B. Kent.

Former Judge Kent (more on his "former" status below) deserves a special aside, as he is as famous for his benchslaps as he is infamous for his non-judicial conduct. He presided for eighteen years over the single-judge Galveston Division of the Southern District of Texas, which spans Brazoria, Chambers, Galveston and Matagorda Counties, and during that time he developed a reputation for published opinions that were both humorous and ridiculing. Many of those opinions were in response to hopeless motions to escape his courtroom. For example:

> Manifestly, any person with even a correspondence-course level understanding of federal practice and procedure would recognize that Defendant's Motion [to transfer venue] is patently insipid, ludicrous and utterly and unequivocally without any merit whatsoever ... Defendant's obnoxiously ancient, boilerplate, inane Motion is emphatically DENIED. Moreover, Defendant's present counsel-of-record, Mr. [redacted] is determined to be disqualified for cause from this action for submitting this asinine tripe.[19]

Former Judge Kent even had stern words for litigants who *wanted* to be in his courtroom. The excerpt below is his unsolicited response to the Republic of Bolivia's decision to bring an action against Phillip Morris Companies in federal court in Texas:

> The Court seriously doubts whether Brazoria County has ever seen a live Bolivian . . . even on the Discovery Channel . . . [T]his humble Court by the sea is certainly flattered by what must be the worldwide renown of rural Texas courts for dispensing justice with unparalleled fairness and alacrity, apparently in common discussion even on the mountain peaks of Bolivia … Plaintiff has an embassy in Washington D.C. … whereas there isn't even a Bolivian restaurant anywhere near here![20]

Former Judge Kent was equally impatient with those who belonged inside his courtroom and wanted out and those who belonged outside his courtroom and wanted in. It is his following response to a request for transfer of venue that provides this country's most well-known example of venue benchslappery:

> Defendant's request for a transfer of venue is centered around the fact that Galveston does not have a commercial airport into which Defendant's employees and corporate representatives may fly and out of which they may be expediently whisked to the federal courthouse in Galveston. Rather, Defendant contends that it will be faced with the huge "inconvenience" of flying into Houston and driving less than forty miles to the Galveston courthouse, an act that will "encumber" it with "unnecessary driving time and expenses."

The Court certainly does not wish to encumber any litigant with such an onerous burden. The court, being somewhat familiar with the Northeast, notes that perceptions about travel are different in that part of the country than they are in Texas. A litigant in that part of the country could cross several states in a few hours and might be shocked at having to travel fifty miles to try a case, but in this vast state of Texas, such a travel distance would not be viewed with any surprise or consternation. [Footnote 1: The sun come up, and the sun done set, but we is still in Texas yet.] Defendant should be assured that it is not embarking on a three-week-long trip via covered wagons when it travels to Galveston. Rather, Defendant will be pleased to discover that the highway is paved and lighted all the way to Galveston, and thanks to the efforts of this Court's predecessor, Judge Roy Bean, the trip should be free of rustlers, hooligans, or vicious varmints of unsavory kind. Moreover, the speed limit was recently increased to seventy miles per hour on most of the road leading to Galveston, so Defendant should be able to hurtle to justice at lightning speed ... The Court notes that any inconvenience suffered in having to drive to Galveston may likely be offset by the peacefulness of the ride and the scenic beauty of the sunny isle...

> "Defendant will be pleased to discover that the highway is lighted all the way to Galveston ... [and] free of rustlers, hooligans, or vicious varmints of unsavory kind."

Defendant argues that flight travel is available between Houston and San Antonio but it is not available between Galveston and San Antonio, again because of the absence of a commercial airport. Alas, this Court's kingdom for a commercial airport! [Footnote 2: Defendant will again be pleased to know that regular limousine service is available from Hobby Airport, even to the steps of this humble courthouse, which has got lights, indoor plummin', 'lectric doors, and all sorts of new stuff, almost like them big courthouses back East.] This Court is unpersuaded by this argument because it is not this Court's concern how Plaintiff gets here, whether it be by plane, train, automobile, horseback, foot, or on the back of a huge Texas jackrabbit, as long as Plaintiff is here at the proper date and time…[21]

Judge Samuel Kent, USDC,
Southern District of Texas

———————————

The incomparable and incorrigible former Judge Kent wouldn't let lawyers out of his courtroom without good reason, and he held counsel to an exacting, perhaps unrealistic standard. His opinions should have been enough to put any attorney on notice as to what to expect in the Galveston Division and to steer clear of that venue whenever possible.

Because of Judge Kent's reputation for benchslaps, litigators in the Southern District of Texas were likely relieved when he resigned from the Bench on June 30, 2009. Those who suffered at his hands may also have felt some vindication in that Mr. Kent's resignation came after his indictment on six federal criminal counts, including sexual assault and obstruction of justice, impeachment by the U.S. Senate and sentencing to 33 months in federal prison.[22] Based on the judge's history of benchslaps, one can only imagine what the lawyers who suffered under him must have thought when they learned of his sentencing. They had plenty of fodder.

Former Judge Kent was referred to as a "drunken giant" by one of the female employees he allegedly groped, and he "bragged" about his ability to intimidate.[23] During sentencing, he issued a self-immolating benchslap when he admitted to being "flawed, selfish, [and] indulgent," and apologized to his wife, family and accusers.[24] Perhaps that apology should have extended to the attorneys who appeared before him. In a moment of poetic justice, Mr. Kent later received a benchslap of his own from Judge Roger Vinson: "Your wrongful conduct is a huge black X, a smear on the legal profession, a stain on the judicial system itself..."[25] At the time of this printing, Mr. Kent is serving out his sentence in state prison in Florida.[26]

Research Judges

As important as it is to research venue, it is critical to research a judge before submitting a brief or appearing before her. It is the minutia that can make or break a case when dealing with judicial authorities. How does the judge feel about *ex parte* applications or continuances? How firm are the judge's tentative opinions? Does the judge place greater emphasis on substantive merits or procedural issues? This information is essential for attorneys to advocate effectively. Unfortunately, not every lawyer takes time to conduct proper research. The lawyers identified in the following opinion erred by failing to understand how important court rules and procedure are to Judge Richard Posner and the Seventh Circuit (and, in truth, to most appellate courts across all jurisdictions):

…The appellees' jurisdictional statement begins promisingly by stating that the appellants' jurisdictional statement "is neither complete [n]or correct." But neither, it turns out, is the appellees'. It does not mention the amount in controversy, erroneously alleged in the appellants' statement; and concerning citizenship it violates Rule 28(a)(1) by stating that the appellees are "citizens of a different state" from the appellants, without indicating what state they are citizens of. It turns out that the insurance company is actually a citizen of a foreign country, so that the relevant provision of the diversity statute, unmentioned in either jurisdictional statement, is 28 U.S.C. § 1332(a)(2).

We asked the parties to submit supplemental jurisdictional statements. The appellants' supplemental statement corrects the omission of Mazda's principal place of business (also California), but blunders with respect to the insurance company by stating that it is "a corporation organized under the laws of Japan with a United States branch domiciled in the State of New York with its principal place of business located at 230 Park Ave, New York, NY 10169." The location of a branch office is irrelevant to diversity jurisdiction. But reference to "domicile" and "principal place of business" naturally raises the question, unaddressed in the statement, whether this branch might be a corporation having its principal place of business in New York but incorporated elsewhere, such as Wisconsin.

We might have expected the blunder to be corrected by the major Chicago law firm representing the appellees. No such luck. Its supplemental jurisdictional statement repeats that the insurance company "is a foreign corporation organized under the laws of Japan with a U.S. Branch. The principal place of business of the U.S. Branch is New York, New York." The fact that "Branch" is capitalized and its principal place of business alleged suggests that it might be a corporation, but at argument the appellees' lawyer said no, it's just a branch. When asked by one of the judges why then it was mentioned in the jurisdictional statement, the lawyer replied inconsequently that "with a U.S. Branch" is Japanese corporate lingo.

The appellees' supplemental jurisdictional statement contains two further errors. ...

We are satisfied that the parties' errors in regard to the amount in controversy are harmless ... But the lawyers have wasted our time as well as their own and (depending on the fee arrangements) their clients' money. We have been plagued by the carelessness of a number of the lawyers practicing before the courts of this circuit with regard to the required contents of jurisdictional statements in diversity cases.

> "[T]he lawyers have wasted our time as well as their own and [depending on the fee arrangements] their clients' money."

It is time, as we noted in BondPro, that this malpractice stopped. We direct the parties to show cause within 10 days why counsel should not be sanctioned for violating Rule 28(a)(1) and mistaking the requirements of diversity jurisdiction. We ask them to consider specifically the appropriateness, as a sanction, of their being compelled to attend a continuing legal education class in federal jurisdiction.

Are we being fusspots and nitpickers in trying (so far with limited success) to enforce rules designed to ensure that federal courts do not exceed the limits that the Constitution and federal statutes impose on their jurisdiction? Does it really matter if federal courts decide on the merits cases that they are not actually authorized to decide? The sky will not fall if federal courts occasionally stray outside the proper bounds. But the fact that limits on subject-matter jurisdiction are not waivable or forfeitable–that federal courts are required to police their jurisdiction–imposes a duty of care that we are not at liberty to shirk. And since we are not investigative bodies, we need and must assure compliance with procedures designed to compel parties to federal litigation to assist us in keeping within bounds. ...

> "Are we being fusspots and nitpickers in trying (so far with limited success) to enforce rules?"

It would be delightful, but irresponsible in the extreme, for us to ignore the limits on our jurisdiction, forget the rules intended to prevent us from ignoring those limits, direct the Clerk of the court to tear out the parties' jurisdictional statements before distributing the briefs to us, and jump directly to the merits of any case that the parties would like to litigate in federal court. . . [27]

Judge Richard Posner, Seventh Circuit

_____

Failure to appreciate the importance of court rules and procedure to the Seventh Circuit resulted in a stern, 1,300 word benchslap. Counsel might have prevented embarrassment if they had done their research. As observed by Ted Frank, legal blogger and former Seventh Circuit Law Clerk: "Ironically, while both parties' attorneys were lambasted for failing to comply precisely with technical and arcane (albeit important) requirements, it was entirely shrugged off that the plaintiff had filed a complaint alleging defectively designed airbags without any supporting evidence. The only consequence for that action was the straightforward affirmance of the summary judgment for the defendants. The contrast of what is and isn't considered a sanctionable waste of the court's and attorneys' time is enlightening."[28] Enlightening indeed, especially to future attorneys appearing before Judge Posner and the Seventh Circuit.

Cite Accurate Legal Authority

Benchslaps for procedural violations are common, but many attorneys are smacked down for far more substantive mistakes. It should go without saying that attorneys must support their arguments with legal authority. Clearly, they should also verify the accuracy of their citations. Two hapless lawyers learned this lesson the hard way in former Judge Kent's courtroom:

> ... Before proceeding further, the Court notes that this case involves two extremely likable lawyers, who have together delivered some of the most amateurish pleadings ever to cross the hallowed causeway into Galveston, an effort which leads

the Court to surmise but one plausible explanation. Both attorneys have obviously entered into a secret pact - complete with hats, handshakes and cryptic words - to draft their pleadings entirely in crayon on the back sides of gravy-stained paper place mats, in the hope that the Court would be so charmed by their child-like efforts that their utter dearth of legal authorities in their briefing would go unnoticed. Whatever actually occurred, the Court is now faced with the daunting task of deciphering their submissions.

With Big Chief tablet readied, thick black pencil in hand, and a devil-may-care laugh in the face of death, life on the razor's edge sense of exhilaration, the Court begins. . . .

Defendant begins the descent into Alice's Wonderland by submitting a Motion that relies upon only one legal authority. The Motion cites a Fifth Circuit case which stands for the whopping proposition that a federal court sitting in Texas applies the Texas statutes of limitations to certain state and federal law claims. That is all well and good — the Court is quite fond of the Erie doctrine; indeed there is talk of little else around both the Canal and this Court's water cooler. Defendant, however, does not even cite to Erie, but to a mere successor case, and further fails to even begin to analyze why the Court should approach the shores of Erie.

Finally, Defendant does not even provide a cite to its desired Texas limitation statute. A more bumbling approach is difficult to conceive — but wait folks. There's More!

> "A more bumbling approach is difficult to conceive – but wait folks. There's More!"

Defendant submitted a Reply brief, on June 11, 2001, after the Court had already drafted, but not finalized, this Order. In a regretful effort to be thorough, the Court reviewed this submission. It too fails to cite to either the Texas statute of limitations or any Fifth Circuit cases discussing maritime law liability for Plaintiff's claims versus Phillips.

Plaintiff responds to this deft, yet minimalist analytical wizardry with an equally gossamer wisp of an argument, although Plaintiff does at least cite the federal limitations provision applicable to maritime tort claims. Naturally, Plaintiff also neglects to provide any analysis whatsoever of why his claim versus Defendant Phillips is a maritime action. Instead, Plaintiff "cites" to a single case from the Fourth Circuit.

Plaintiff's citation, however, points to a nonexistent Volume "1886" of the Federal Reporter Third Edition and neglects to provide a pinpoint citation for what, after being located, turned out to be a forty-page decision. Ultimately, to the Court's dismay after reviewing the opinion, it stands simply for the bombshell proposition that torts committed on navigable waters (in this case an alleged defamation committed by the controversial G. Gordon Liddy aboard a cruise ship at sea) require the application of general maritime rather than state tort law. *See Wells v. Liddy,* 186 F.3d 505, 524 (Fourth Cir. 1999) (What the ...)?!

"(What the ...)?!"

The Court cannot even begin to comprehend why this case was selected for reference. It is almost as if Plaintiff's counsel chose the opinion by throwing long range darts at the Federal

Reporter (remarkably enough hitting a nonexistent volume!). And though the Court often gives great heed to dicta from courts as far flung as those of Manitoba, it finds this case unpersuasive. There is nothing in Plaintiff's cited case about ingress or egress between a vessel and a dock, although counsel must have been thinking that Mr. Liddy must have had both ingress and egress from the cruise ship at some docking facility, before uttering his fateful words.

Further, as noted above, Plaintiff has submitted a Supplemental Opposition to Defendant's Motion. This Supplement is longer than Plaintiff's purported Response, cites more cases, several constituting binding authority from either the Fifth Circuit or the Supreme Court, and actually includes attachments which purport to be evidence. However, this is all that can be said positively for Plaintiff's Supplement, which does nothing to explain why, on the facts of this case, Plaintiff has an admiralty claim against Phillips (which probably makes some sense because Plaintiff doesn't).

Plaintiff seems to rely on the fact that he has pled Rule 9(h) and stated an admiralty claim versus the vessel and his employer to demonstrate that maritime law applies to Phillips. This bootstrapping argument does not work; Plaintiff must properly invoke admiralty law versus each Defendant discretely. Despite the continued shortcomings of Plaintiff's supplemental submission, the Court commends Plaintiff for his vastly improved choice of crayon — Brick Red is much easier on the eyes than Goldenrod, and stands out much better amidst the mustard splotched about Plaintiff's briefing. But at the end of the day, even if you put a calico dress on it and call it Florence, a pig is still a pig.

Now, alas, the Court must return to grownup land. As vaguely alluded to by the parties, the issue in this case turns upon which law — state or maritime — applies to each of Plaintiff's potential claims versus Defendant Phillips. And despite Plaintiff's and Defendant's joint, heroic efforts to obscure it, the answer to this question is readily ascertained. . .

After this remarkably long walk on a short legal pier, having received no useful guidance whatever from either party, the Court has endeavored, primarily based upon its affection for both counsel, but also out of its own sense of morbid curiosity, to resolve what it perceived to be the legal issue presented. Despite the waste of perfectly good crayon seen in both parties' briefing (and the inexplicable odor of wet dog emanating from such) the Court believes it has satisfactorily resolved this matter. Defendant's Motion for Summary Judgment is GRANTED.

> "Despite the waste of a perfectly good crayon seen in both parties' briefing (and the inexplicable odor of wet dog emanating from such) the Court believes it has satisfactorily resolved this matter."

At this juncture, Plaintiff retains, albeit seemingly to his befuddlement and/or consternation, a maritime law cause of action versus his alleged Jones Act employer, Defendant Unity Marine Corporation, Inc. However, it is well known around these parts that Unity Marine's lawyer is equally likable and has been writing crisply in ink since the second grade. Some old-timers even spin yarns of an ability to type. The Court cannot speak to the veracity of such loose talk, but out of caution, the

Court suggests that Plaintiff's lovable counsel had best upgrade to a nice shiny No. 2 pencil or at least sharpen what's left of the stubs of his crayons for what remains of this heart-stopping, spine-tingling action.

In either case, the Court cautions Plaintiff's counsel not to run with a sharpened writing utensil in hand — he could put his eye out. [29]

Judge Samuel Kent, USDC,
Southern District of Texas

————————————

Attorneys should beware that it is not always enough to cite supporting legal authority. Judges also expect counsel to address and distinguish contrary legal authority. In *Thul v. Onewest*, one of the most highly regarded litigators in the country was humiliated by District Court Judge Matthew Kennelly when he failed to do just that.

The attorneys who submitted OneWest's opening brief, John Beisner and Jessica Miller of the Washington, D.C. office of Skadden, Arps, Slate, Meagher & Flom, LLP, and Andrew Fuchs of the Chicago office of that firm, ought to have brought *Wigod* to the Court's attention in their opening brief. Their failure to do so almost certainly ran afoul of their obligation of candor under ABA Model Rule of Professional Conduct 3.3(a)(2) and the corresponding District of Columbia (D.C. RPC 3.3(a)(3)) and Illinois rules (Ill. RPC 3.3(a)(2)), and it likely amounted to conduct sanctionable under Federal Rule of Civil Procedure 11(b)(2) and 28 U.S.C. § 1927. The Court will address this point further at the end of this decision …

The Court also directs each of the attorneys who submitted the motion to dismiss and supporting briefs, John Beisner, Jessica Miller, and Andrew Fuchs of the law firm of Skadden, Arps, Slate, Meagher & Flom, LLP, to show cause in writing, by no later than January 10, 2013, why they should not be sanctioned in one or more of the following ways: (a) payment of plaintiffs' reasonable attorney's fees and expenses caused by advancing arguments contrary to the Seventh Circuit's *Wigod* decision without bringing that case to the Court's attention; (b) revocation of the *pro hac vice* status of Mr. Beisner and Ms. Miller; (c) a written and/or oral reprimand; (d) any other sanction that may be appropriate. The ruling date of January 3, 2013 is vacated. The case is set for a status hearing in open court on January 17, 2013 at 9:30 a.m. Mr. Beisner, Ms. Miller, and Mr. Fuchs are all directed to appear in person.[30]

The "Mr. Beisner" identified in the opinion above was none other than John Beisner, then co-head of Skadden's mass torts and insurance litigation group, one of the most prestigious partners of one of the most prestigious practice groups in the country.[31] Mr. Beisner was also once considered a candidate for the chairmanship of the equally prestigious O'Melveny & Myers.[32] His public shaming is yet another reminder that no attorney is immune to benchslaps.

Mr. Beisner et al's response was filed on January 10, 2013, and aside from a clear and profuse apology to the court, it contains one paragraph worth reprinting here:

Mr. Beisner and Ms. Miller further wish to clarify that they had ultimate responsibility for the legal briefing in this matter. Mr. Fuchs was neither the principal drafter of the briefs nor tasked with conducting research related to the briefs. While Mr. Fuchs reviewed the opening brief prior to its filing, he relied upon Mr. Beisner and Ms. Miller with respect to the legal content of the briefing and was not personally aware of the *Wigod* decision.[33]

While benchslaps are amusing, it is important to remember the devastating effect they can have on the careers of attorneys. Mr. Beisner and Ms. Miller, whose careers and reputations can withstand the embarrassment, should be commended for falling on their swords and accepting the full brunt of Judge Kennelly's displeasure. Luckily, Mr. Fuchs did not share in Mr. Beisner's and Ms. Miller's fate.

[T]he Court vacates the order to show cause as to Mr. Fuchs. In the attorneys' written response, they stated that Mr. Fuchs "was neither the principal drafter of the briefs nor tasked with conducting research related to the briefs"; he relied on the other two attorneys concerning the legal content of the briefing; and he was not personally aware of the Seventh Circuit decision in question.... Mr. Fuchs is an associate, and the other lawyers are senior to him. The Court accepts the attorneys' statement and vacates the show cause order as it relates to Mr. Fuchs.[34]

As readers will discover in later chapters, not all junior attorneys are so lucky.

Don't Interrupt the Judge _____

Some judges, who shall remain nameless, enjoy the sound of their own voices. Some judges also lose their temper in open court. A combination of the two can be lethal. New York Civil Court Judge Walter Tolub is said to have interrupted an attorney once to pose a question: "If you stopped talking, do you think you'd die?"[35] In short, when appearing in court, attorneys should speak only when necessary, answer judges' questions directly and never – *never* – interrupt the judge.

This is no joke. Los Angeles Superior Court Judge Joan Comparet-Cassani allegedly ordered a litigant shocked with 50,000 volts of electricity for repeated interruptions,[36] and some judges instruct bailiffs to keep a thick roll of duct tape on-hand for chronic interrupters.[37] It may seem like common sense not to interrupt a judge in open court, but it's easy to forget this bit of wisdom in the heat of the moment. For example, during a lively hearing that preceded dismissal of an SEC lawsuit, government lawyer Catherine Pappas earned the distinction of being instructed to "sit down and shut up" in open court by a federal judge:

> **Judge Mullen:** Why in the world don't you all make [naked short selling] illegal? Don't you understand what happens in the market when you allow naked short selling to attack companies? I mean, do you understand that?
> **Greer:** Your Honor, I think that that's an issue for the United States Congress. I appreciate your concern –
> **Judge Mullen:** Well –
> **Greer:** — and I –

46

Judge Mullen: — the answer to my question is, yeah, I understand it or, no, I don't.

Greer: I do understand your –

Judge Mullen: Do not try — okay.

Greer: I do understand, Your Honor.

Judge Mullen: Thank you for understanding it.

Covington: Your Honor, one thing –

Judge Mullen: Excuse the interruption.

Covington: No, sir.

Judge Mullen: Sit down, shut up, let the man talk. I'm not going to let him introduce (sic) you. Last warning.

> "Sit down, shut up, let the man talk."

Pappas: I'm sorry?

Judge Mullen: Sit down –

Pappas: Yeah, I got that.

Judge Mullen: — shut up, let the man talk. Last warning.

Pappas: Okay.

Judge Mullen: Understood?

Pappas: Okay.

Judge Mullen: Excellent.

Covington: With all due respect, Your Honor –

Judge: And you don't interrupt her when she's talking.

Covington: Yes, sir.

Judge: Proceed.[38]

Judge Graham Mullen, USDC,
Western District of North Carolina

———————————

The above transcript highlights another useful nugget of wisdom: never begin a sentence, "With all due respect, your honor..." You might as well wave a red flag before an angry bull.

Don't Invite Trouble _____

A corollary of "don't interrupt" is a childhood maxim of equal importance: speak only when spoken to. Speaking up when uninvited draws attention, and rarely in a good way.

In a prominent perjury case involving former Vice-President Dick Cheney's chief of staff, Judge Reggie Walton sentenced Lewis "Scooter" Libby to 30 months in prison. In response to the sentencing, a group of twelve prominent legal scholars filed a motion requesting permission to file an *amicus* brief in the case. According to *The Washington Post*, Judge Walton responded in mere hours with a one-page order granting the motion, but he included the following footnote, described by one commentator as "an instant classic in the annals of judicial footnotes."[39]

It is an impressive show of public service when twelve prominent and distinguished current and former law professors of well-respected schools are able to amass their collective wisdom in the course of only several days to provide their legal expertise to the Court on behalf of a criminal defendant. The Court trusts that this is a reflection of these eminent academics' willingness in the future to step up to the plate and provide like assistance in cases involving any of the numerous litigants, both in this Court and throughout the courts of our nation, who lack the financial means to fully and properly articulate the merits of their legal positions even in instances where failure to do so could result in monetary penalties, incarceration or worse. The court will certainly not hesitate to call for assistance from these luminaries, as necessary in the interest of justice and equity, whenever similar questions arise in the cases that come before it.[40]

Who signed the brief? A dream team of legal academics, including Robert Bork, Alan Dershowitz, Vikram Amar of Hastings Law, Randy Barnett and Viet Dinh of Georgetown Law; Douglas Kmiec and Robert Pushaw of Pepperdine Law, Richard Parker of Harvard Law, Gary Lawson of Boston University Law, Thomas Merrill of Columbia Law, Earl Maltz of Rutgers-Camden Law and Robert Nagel of Colorado Law. Since they chose to enter the legal fray uninvited, they cannot complain at being singled out by Judge Walton. One only hopes they took his admonition to heart.

Attorney Therese Cesar Garza, a former public defender in Illinois, provides another cautionary tale about unsolicited interjections. When Ms. Cesar failed to produce her client at trial, Cook County Circuit Court Judge Anthony Calabrese issued a warrant for her client's arrest. Ms. Cesar's subsequent outburst prompted the following exchange.

Ms. Cesar: Oh shit!
Judge Calabrese: What did you say, Ms. Cesar?
Ms. Cesar: Oh shoot, I said. Oh shoot. I'm sorry I didn't talk to her, Judge. I'm just – it's my fault. I'm running around, talking to people.
Judge Calabrese: I don't think that's what you said.

Ms. Cesar: Whatever. I know the word you think I said. My mother never let me say that, and I'll tell you why. But I said shoot, darn it. …

Judge Calabrese: Let me just indicate again, you are yelling on the record. This happens all the time when you don't get your way. Because you lose something doesn't mean you have to start yelling at me. I haven't gotten deaf over the course of the time I have listened to your argument.[41]

Ms. Cesar's unfortunate outburst resulted in formal disciplinary proceedings before her state's Commission, along with the national notoriety that comes with headlining several legal blogs. Her experience should be a lesson to all attorneys regarding the wisdom of simply remaining silent.

Read and Research before Signing

It may seem beneath mentioning that practitioners should read and understand documents before signing them. However, in some law firms and legal departments, documents pass through many hands before they are ultimately signed and filed. This is especially common in very large organizations where the person whose name appears on the caption is rarely the person who performed the initial research and drafting. Some partners and senior counsel rely heavily on associates or more junior attorneys to prepare work product. When senior attorneys do take a "hands-on" role in a case, they may lack familiarity with the facts or procedural history that was previously the province of junior staff.

On October 31, 2007, U.S. District Court Judge Paul L. Friedman issued the following benchslap to the District of Columbia in a case over school funding: "The defendants' response demonstrates a stunning ignorance of the history of [the] litigation and the operative orders by this court … The only plausible explanation is that the attorneys whose names appear on the signature page … *must not have read it.*"[42] One can assume Judge Friedman was being facetious, but his warning may ring true to many practitioners, particularly those at large firms. The simple lesson? Read and research before signing.

File Only Necessary Documents and Eggs _____

Attorneys conceive myriad ways to present arguments, and creativity is an asset to any practitioner. However, just as art is in the eye of the beholder, so too is evidence in the eyes of a judge and jury. Florida attorney Jack Thompson forgot this adage when he attached gay pornographic images to a motion he filed in federal district court.

Jack Thompson has a colorful history. He is well-known within the media and technology sectors for his vociferous, unmitigated and sometimes unintelligible opposition to sex and violence in video games. He doesn't stop there. His stance extends to opposing obscenity in modern culture more generally, including in rap music, pornography, radio, film and television. (Note that Mr. Thompson's definition of what constitutes an "obscenity" may not reflect most mainstream definitions.) Within the legal community, Mr. Thompson is best known for his bizarre court filings and nearly unparalleled willingness to insult the Bench and the Bar, both of which he has accused of corruption and incompetence.

Because of Mr. Thompson's notoriety, U.S. District Court Judge Adalberto Jordan of the Southern District of Florida should not have been surprised when Mr. Thompson made outlandish and unorthodox legal arguments in his courtroom. But even with that expectation, he was shocked when Mr. Thompson filed several graphic examples of gay pornography with the court and then accused opposing counsel of peddling those images to children. Judge Jordan was not persuaded by Mr. Thompson's "evidence," and he issued the following order:

On September 19, 2007, Mr. Thompson – who is the plaintiff in this case and an attorney by profession – filed a motion for leave to file a document, and attached an exhibit to that motion. The attached exhibit, which includes several graphic images of oral and genital sex between adult males, was filed electronically in the docket in this case, without prior permission from the court, and it was not filed under seal. Mr. Thompson filed these images – in a place where they are available for viewing by members of the public, including children – notwithstanding his knowledge of their offensive nature. In fact, Mr. Thompson himself found the images to be so offensive that they were the subject of a request on his part to the Florida Bar to prosecute the attorney who allegedly provided links to the images on his law firm's website.

"No court need tolerate the use of obscene, indecent, and scandalous pleadings." *Adams v. Nankervis*, 902 F.2d 1578 (Table), 1990 WL 61990, at *3 (Ninth Cir. 1990). The graphic images Mr. Thompson attached to his motion are indecent, obscene, and offensive. To the extent that the other attorney's alleged conduct is in any way relevant to the claims in Mr. Thompson's third amended complaint, there was no need for Mr. Thompson to file these graphic images in the public record. A simple reference to the website and its alleged links would have sufficed. At the very least, Mr. Thompson should have filed the graphic images under seal or sought the court's permission to file the images in the public record. Through his actions, Mr. Thompson made available for unlimited public viewing, on the court's docketing system, these graphic images. For this reason, by October 5, 2007, Mr. Thompson shall show cause why this incident should not be referred to the court's Ad Hoc Committee on Attorney Admissions, Peer Review, and Attorney Grievance for appropriate action. [43]

> Judge Adalberto Jordan, USDC,
> Southern District of Florida

――――――――――――――――

Between September 25 and October 1, Mr. Thompson filed nineteen separate responses to Judge Jordan's order to show cause, an average of 3.8 filings per business day. These responses contained a meandering series of allegations about the court, opposing counsel and numerous other individuals and institutions.

In the interest of helping readers understand why some judges are induced to benchslap counsel, excerpts from a single one of those nineteen responses, captioned "Verified Motion to Vacate Order to Show Cause," is reproduced below. The author encourages readers to contemplate how they might respond if presented with nineteen similar filings over a seven day span.

COMES NOW plaintiff, John B. Thompson, hereinafter Thompson, as an attorney on his own behalf, and moves this court to vacate its September 24 order to show cause, pursuant to Rule 60 (b), Federal Rules of Civil Procedure, stating:

THE COURT'S UNDERSTANDABLE MISTAKE AND ERROR

1. This Honorable Court entered its September 24 Order to Show Cause because of its concern that these "obscene" images could now be seen by "members of the public, even children." Plaintiff rightly assumes, given the acumen of this court, particularly when it comes to as dangerous a remedy as contempt, that it chose its words carefully. Thompson takes the court at its word when it based its concern solely upon the allegation that Thompson had made these images available to "members of the public, even children."

2. Rule 60 (b), FRCP, provides for vacating an order based upon mistake. The court, with all respect and in fact because of the respect Thompson has for it/him, and the federal judicial system, notes that the court has made an erroneous assumption and then based its show cause order on that understandable error. . . .

7. The court, then, has based its contempt effort upon Thompson's alleged exposure of obscenity to the public and "children," and in doing so it has made a "mistake," within the meaning of Rule 60 (b), as the court possibly was thinking that

Thompson had gone deep into the recesses of some adult, restricted zone of the Internet, obtained this material, and then inserted it into the court file where "children" could then, for the first time, see it. Nothing could be further from the truth. One of the signal failings of the Bush Justice Department and one of the reasons that pro-family, pro-values organizations feel betrayed by this Administration is the extent to which this Administration has failed to prosecute obscenity, especially on the Internet, where it has grown like topsy, which has made tragic events such as the recent arrest of a Florida US Attorney, Mr. Atchison, more likely.

8. Any American who does not understand that pornography, of whatever kind, on the Internet, is making the "sex trade" in people of all ages more likely and more easily effectuated has no idea what is going on in America. . . .

10. In 1982, two residents of what was then called Dade County, Florida, videotaped poll workers illegally pre-punching computer punch card ballots since abandoned as ballots by Florida after the "hanging chad" Presidential election chaos of 2000.

11. These two residents took this videotape of this vote fraud by poll workers along with a box of the tampered with punch cards to then Dade County State Attorney Janet Reno. What did Janet Reno do? She arrested these two men for "stealing ballots" and charged them with a crime. In doing so, Reno charged with a crime the two men who had brought her evidence of the commission of a crime. The court or anyone can read all about it in the book Votescam available at Amazon.com at http://www.amazon.com/Votescam-Stealing-James-M-

Collier/dp/0963416308. [The next two paragraphs involve Ms. Reno and her alleged misconduct.] . . .

14. What did plaintiff herein do that has this court now seeking a criminal contempt finding against him? He took evidence of a crime to this court the best way he knew how, and the fact that this court has come face to face with the best evidence of this criminal activity is proof that Thompson's methodology worked. The court has been so struck by what it has seen that it has labeled this material which a Florida-licensed lawyer is providing to anyone of any age on a commercial site "obscene," as that term is used in *Miller v. California.* Thompson genuinely thanks this court for having had the perspicacity and courage to call this swill what it is.

15. Thompson submits that it is more than likely that if Thompson had submitted merely the links to this sewage that Mr. Kent is superintending for commercial gain, then the court would not have seen the material. Sometimes it is hard to ignore something that one sees, as the President of Iran, as Thompson has already pointed out, needs to see images from Dachau, Austerlitiz, and Treblinka.

16. The Florida Bar, which has a cottage industry going protecting Norm Kent, Tew Cardenas, Blank Rome, The Howard Stern Show, Take-Two Interactive's Grand Theft Auto, and the commercial assault upon other people's children, while at the same time threatening to disbar Thompson for his whistleblower status, could not care less about the commercial exploitation of children. . . .

22. The above makes it clear that this court understands the problem of sex trafficking. Thompson has been working on this problem since 1987, back when Mr. Kent was representing someone whom the Adam Walsh Foundation concluded, in its letter to the FCC, sent at Thompson's request, "was soliciting teenaged boys for sex on the public airwaves through his radio program." Mr. Kent, then, has a long history with this "porn in the public square" phenomenon.

23. Thompson has had the pleasure of sharing the podium with Ronald Reagan's Attorney General Edwin Meese, whose Commission on Pornography pinned the pornography tail on the sex trade donkey. Possibly US Attorney Acosta, who has looked the other way as to obscenity trafficking, would do well to read the Meese Commission Report and conclude, as did the undersigned twenty years ago, that in order to do more about the Kent Franks of this world we need to do something—anything—about the purveyors of crap like www.justboys.com. Thompson has tried to be consistent on this problem, which is why he sent the material he did to this court and why The Florida Bar, with its bizarre pro-porn, anti-Christian agenda, has singled Thompson out for harassment for twenty years.

24. Thompson was not trying to tear down this court. He was appealing to it to do something. No one else has. Thompson would ask this court to contact U.S. Attorney Acosta and ask him to do something, rather than killing investigations about this in their infancy.

WHEREFORE, Thompson respectfully asks this court to vacate its Order to Show Cause because of the understandable mistake it apparently made in assuming that Thompson made this obscene material available to "children" from a place that it had been sequestered from children. Nothing could be further from the truth. To proceed against Thompson criminally for his having alerted the federal judicial system of this criminal activity, and The Bar's collaboration in it, would be akin to prosecuting a citizen who has found child pornography, where children can get it, to a police station—for that citizen's "possession of child pornography." Janet Reno did the equivalent of that already, and it didn't work out. Plaintiff respectfully suggest that for this court to use its contempt power against Thompson vitiates the perceived fairness of these underlying proceedings, and it threatens to turn Thompson from a porn industry nuisance into an unwilling hero of American parents everywhere. The headline this court should wish to avoid:

"PORN-AGAIN" ANTI-SMUT CRUSADER JAILED BY BUSH APPOINTED FEDERAL JUDGE FOR BRINGING EVIDENCE OF OBSCENITY TRAFFICKING TO COURT; ATTORNEY JACK THOMPSON SET TO APPEAR ON FOX NEWS CHANNEL'S THE O'REILLY FACTOR TONIGHT... [44]

Now, readers should imagine reading the additional 2,000 words that were omitted from the above pleading, along with eighteen similar filings, and all during a span of five days, in addition to the regular law, motion and trial practice that goes on in a federal courtroom. Judge Jordan was not amused by Mr. Thompson's responses or threats. He issued this succinct order on October 1, 2007:

Mr. Thompson is hereby advised that the number of documents he has filed in this lawsuit is unreasonable and will not be tolerated going forward. For example, in the last week alone, Mr. Thompson filed 13 different documents in response to a single show cause order. This case has only been pending for four months, and has not even moved beyond the motion to dismiss stage, yet Mr. Thompson has already filed 74 separate motions, notices, and other pleadings. By comparison, the

> "[In four months], Mr. Thompson has already filed 74 separate motions, notices, and other pleadings."

two defendants put together have only filed 11 documents (and most of those were motions to dismiss which the defendants were forced to file, and refile, on account of Mr. Thompson's repeated amendments to his complaint).

While Mr. Thompson has the right to request relief from the court when necessary, his role as a litigant in this lawsuit does not give him free reign to unnecessarily flood the docket in this case with motions and other documents, especially when the filings have no bearing on the issues in dispute in this case. Despite what Mr. Thompson may think, this case is not a war

> "Despite what Mr. Thompson may think, this case is not a war with the world regarding the state of its moral standards."

with the world regarding the state of its moral standards (if it is, I clearly do not have jurisdiction). Therefore, he cannot continue to use this case as platform to battle everything in society with which he disagrees.

Accordingly, going forward, Mr. Thompson must limit his filings in this case. Specifically, if a response is requested of him, he shall file one (1) document, which includes all arguments (and any attachments) that he wishes to present to the court in response. In addition, Mr. Thompson must limit his filings to the issues in dispute in this case, and which are pending before the court.[45]

Judge Adalberto Jordan, USDC,
Southern District of Florida

———————————

Unfortunately for Judge Jordan and the Federal and Florida Justice system, the Jack Thompson saga is ongoing. In early 2008 Thompson was disbarred for five years from the Florida Bar, an organization against which he has a number of long-standing grievances. His disbarment was based on 2,400 pages of transcripts and 1,700 pages of exhibits, and his alleged misconduct included making false statements to tribunals, disparaging and humiliating litigants, making repetitive and frivolous filings and insulting the integrity of the court.[46] The Florida Supreme Court drew attention to one filing that included what Mr. Thompson labeled "a picture book for adults," and contained images of swastikas, kangaroos in court, a reproduced dollar bill, cartoon squirrels, Paul Simon, Paul Newman, Ray Charles, a handprint with the word 'SLAPP' written under it, Bar Governor Benedict P. Kuehne, a baby, Ed Bradley, Jack Nicholson, Justice Clarence Thomas, Julius Caesar, a monkey, a house of cards and other images.[47] Although not reproduced here, the author recommends readers take an opportunity to read Mr. Thompson's "picture book" as an unparalleled example of creativity in filing.

On July 8, 2008, the Florida Supreme Court went one step further and ordered Mr. Thompson permanently disbarred, citing his

> cumulative misconduct, a repeated pattern of behavior relentlessly forced upon numerous unconnected individuals, a total lack of remorse or even slight acknowledgment of inappropriate conduct, and continued behavior consistent with the previous public reprimand … Over a very extended period of time involving a number of totally unrelated cases and individuals, the Respondent has demonstrated a pattern of conduct to strike out harshly, extensively, repeatedly and willfully to simply try to bring as much difficulty, distraction and anguish to those he considers in opposition to his causes … He does not proceed within the guidelines of appropriate professional behavior, but rather uses other means available to intimidate, harass, or bring public disrepute to those whom he perceives oppose him.[48]

Now that's a benchslap.

Even permanent disbarment and a stinging benchslap could not deter Mr. Thompson. In September 2009 he claimed he was "never disbarred" and expressed his intention to resume legal practice. He invited the Florida Bar to seek a court order to stop him.[49] At the time of this printing, there is a motion for reconsideration pending. The docket alone is over 24 pages long.

Despite the entertaining farce of Mr. Thompson's filings and the egregiousness of his filing *faux pas*, even he cannot top a federal court filing by *pro se* litigant Charles Jay Wolff. Mr. Wolff, protesting the diet in a New Hampshire state prison, attached a hard-boiled egg to documents he sent via U.S. Mail to U.S. District Court Judge James Muirhead. That's right, a hard-boiled egg. Judge Muirhead's response to the attachment is so amusing it is reproduced here in its entirety:[50]

```
I do not like eggs in the file.
I do not like them in any style.
I will not take them fried or boiled.
I will not take them poached or broiled.
I will not take them soft or scrambled
Despite an argument well-rambled.

No fan I am.
Of the egg at hand.
Destroy that egg!
Today! Today!
Today I say!  Without delay!
```

SO ORDERED (with apologies to Dr. Seuss).

James R. Muirhead
United States Magistrate Judge

CHAPTER 4: Discovery Disses

It is hard to find more fertile ground for dispute than discovery. Some attorneys see discovery as a high-stakes game, with the goal of appearing forthcoming while at the same time withholding or obscuring as much evidence as possible. In some cases, parties with deep pockets use discovery as a means of burying their opponents in thousands or even millions of documents. Others use discovery to delay litigation, cause inconvenience or increase their opponent's costs. These tactics corrupt a process that was designed to take place without the court's oversight and that relies on the honest and good faith efforts of opposing counsel.

Litigators are understandably skeptical of their opponents' "honest and good faith efforts" without an outside referee to supervise the discovery process. The complexity of e-discovery has only exacerbated this mistrust. And as the cost and uncertainty of trial increases, the majority of civil cases settle immediately in the wake of discovery.[51] As a result, the discovery process has never been more important or contentious.

In a true discovery dispute, each party believes it is being perfectly reasonable and the opposing party utterly irrational. Of course, when discovery disputes require court intervention, judges usually have a different take. For example, Federal Magistrate Judge Peggy Leen was not pleased to rule on a plaintiff's "Emergency Motion to Forbid Improper Objections," and she issued a benchslap neither counsel will likely forget anytime soon.

Before the court is Mazzeo's Emergency Motion to Forbid Attorney Walter Cannon from Making Improper Objections at Depositions and for Sanctions. The court has considered the motion, Defendants' opposition, and Plaintiff's reply.

The parties' multiple discovery disputes in this contentious litigation began even before the parties submitted separate proposed discovery plans. The court has conducted many discovery and dispute resolution hearings and conferences and has considered and decided a dozen or more discovery motions. Thankfully, after several extensions and adjustments, the discovery cutoff has expired. In the current motion Plaintiff seeks an order prohibiting Attorney Walter Cannon from making improper speaking, argumentative, suggestive, and coaching objections during depositions in violation of Rule 30 of the Federal Rules of Civil Procedure. It was filed on an "emergency" basis because Plaintiffs' counsel expected the same problems would arise in two depositions scheduled within days of filing this motion. My practice is to preliminarily review every motion called an "emergency" the day it is filed. However, other cases, motions filed, scheduled hearings and settlement conferences do not afford me the luxury of dropping everything to hear a party's perceived "emergency" especially when it involves a case that has already taken an inordinate amount of the court's time (to the detriment of other litigants who need decisions in their matters) to resolve yet another in a series of routine discovery disputes. Thus, as the motion has worked its way up the tall stack of other matters on my desk, there are no longer any depositions to take. I am not the Maytag repairman of federal judges desperately hoping for something to do. Nevertheless, the motion remains on my docket until an order is entered, and Plaintiff's counsel seeks sanctions. A rough draft of the deposition of Deputy Chief Greg McCurdy is attached as Exhibit "1" to the motion to support the arguments made by Plaintiff's counsel that Mr. Cannon engaged in improper and obstructive conduct for which he deserves to be sanctioned. Plaintiff relies on the provisions of Rule 30(d)(2) which permit the court to impose an appropriate sanction, "including the reasonable expenses and attorneys fees incurred by any party on a person who impedes, delays, or frustrates the fair examination of the deponent." Counsel for Plaintiff asks for attorney's fees and costs incurred for the necessity of filing this motion and "escalating sanctions for further misconduct" if it occurs.

> "I am not the Maytag repairman of federal judges desperately hoping for something to do."

Mr. Cannon filed an opposition to the motion which concedes "that at least some of the subject objections were overly verbose." However, he denies that his "overly verbose" objections were made to coach the witness or for any other improper purpose. He laments that "the objections were made out of frustration over the manner in which Plaintiff's counsel had conducted his depositions over the past fourteen (14) days." Acknowledging there is never an excuse for failing to comply with the Federal Rules of Civil Procedure and the Federal Rules of Evidence, he asks that the Court not impose sanctions. He also attaches excerpts of depositions conducted by counsel for the Plaintiff to support his position that Mr. Kossack engaged in the same objectionable conduct during his client's deposition taking "speaking objections to another level" to coach his client. Other remarks about the conduct of Plaintiff's counsel throughout this case are made which are, at best, unseemly and will not be repeated in this order. Mr. Cannon concludes that "the conduct of defense counsel during these depositions pales in comparison to that of Plaintiff's attorney" and therefore asks that the court deny Plaintiff's request for costs and attorneys' fees. Counsel for Plaintiff could not resist replying. Mr Kossack's reply adds up the number of Mr. Cannon's improper objections during Mr. McCurdy's deposition and compares them to the number of improper objections Mr. Cannon accuses him of making. Not wanting to miss an opportunity to engage in equally unseemly "tit-for-tat," Mr Kossack pads his reply with gratuitous comments which include a reference to counsels' respective choice of beverages during depositions.

> "To ensure that reading the 185 pages of these exchanges was not a complete waste of time, I assigned this motion to a law student extern … he correctly concluded that both lawyers engaged in misconduct."

To ensure that reading the 185 pages of these exchanges was not a complete waste of time, I assigned this motion to a law student extern to prepare a legal memorandum to further his education. In a short period of time he was able to prepare a well-written, concise memo which identified a large number of state and federal cases throughout the country articulating the standards for making deposition objections and identifying improper conduct for which lawyers have been admonished or sanctioned. He correctly concluded that both lawyers engaged in misconduct which violated Rule 30(c)(2).

The exchanges related in excruciating, repetitive detail in the moving and responsive papers and their attachments were painful to read. If I was an elementary school teacher instead of a judge I would require both counsel to write the following clearly established legal rules on a blackboard 500 times: I will not make speaking, coaching, suggestive objections which violate Rule 30(c)(2). I am an experienced lawyer and know that objections must be concise, non- argumentative and non-suggestive. I understand that the purpose of a deposition is to find out what the witness thinks, saw, heard or did. I know that lawyers are not supposed to coach or change the witness's own words to form a legally convenient record. I know I am prohibited from frustrating or impeding the fair examination of a deponent during the deposition. I know that constant objections and unnecessary remarks are unwarranted and frustrate opposing counsel's right to fair examination. I know that speaking objections such as "if you remember," "if you know," "don't guess," "you've answered the question," and "do you understand the question" are designed to coach the witness and are improper. I also know that counsel's interjection that he or she does not understand the question is not a proper objection, and that if a witness needs clarification of a question, the witness may ask for the clarification.

> "[T]hese papers, and the conduct they relate, make me feel like a school marm scolding little boys."

Although these papers, and the conduct they relate, make me feel like a school marm scolding little boys, I am the judge whose duty it is to decide this motion. Accordingly, Mr. Kossack and Mr. Cannon are admonished for engaging in conduct which I know you know violates Rule 30(c)(2). You are better men and better lawyers than the conduct in which you have engaged illustrates.[52]

Peggy A. Leen, USDC, District of Nevada

As demonstrated by Magistrate Judge and "school marm" Peggy Leen, many discovery benchslaps are delivered to attorneys who simply can't get along. Judges are annoyed by these discovery disputes because they prolong litigation unnecessarily. After all, whether it happens today or a month from now, witnesses will eventually get deposed, documents will eventually be produced, interrogatories will eventually be answered. These disputes serve no purpose but to delay.

Unfortunately, "delay, delay, delay" is a common litigation tactic. Many attorneys have become adept at prolonging litigation through the discovery process, including by objecting, requesting extensions, rescheduling depositions, seeking court relief or producing documents on a rolling basis. But as with any time-honored litigation tactic, delay can be taken too far. Chief Judge Royce Lambert of the District of Columbia began his benchslap for e-discovery delay in *DL v. District of Columbia* with the following analogy:

> … Imagine a standup comic who delivers the punch-lines of his jokes first, a plane with landing gear that deploys just after touchdown, or a stick of dynamite with a unique fuse that ignites only after it explodes. That's what document production after trial is like—it defeats the purpose. Yet, the District's Motion would have this Court bless its decision to violate multiple Court orders, ignore the Federal Rules' carefully calibrated discovery apparatus, and produce thousands of responsive e-mails after trial ended. A discovery violation of this exotic magnitude is literally unheard of in this Court, and when—on the first day of trial—the District's plan was revealed, this Court held that the District had waived objections (including privileges) with regard to all of the unproduced e-mail and ordered it to produce them all within one week of the close of trial. Before the Court now is the District's Motion to reconsider that Order. After exploring the relevant aspects of this case's factual background, the Court will explain its reasons for denying the District's Motion. . .

Why does the Court deny the District's Motion? To borrow a common saying, there is a short answer and a long one. The short answer is that the Order is just in light of the District's repeated, flagrant, and unrepentant failures to comply with Court orders. The long answer, which the Court provides below, requires it to explain those failures in detail and to give its reasons for rejecting the District's arguments for reconsideration. First, the Court will explain the District's various discovery obligations and how it violated them. Then, it will show that the District was totally without excuse for those violations. Next, it will discuss its reasons for concluding that there was no practical alternative to the sanctions it imposed. Finally, it will emphasize the deterrence values that guided its decision...

The District should have informed the Court of the problem. It could have filed another motion for an extension of time or a status update to alert the Court to the issue. It could have said something at any of the multiple status conferences held in this case or at the pretrial conference. Instead, the District failed to produce documents for over two years, violated multiple Court Orders in the process, and instead of informing the Court of the situation at any point along the way, it simply sprung the news on the first day of trial. The District's complaints of lack of resources and time pressure fall on deaf ears because it failed to seek relief through any of the Rule-based mechanisms discussed above. Accordingly, it is without excuse... [53]

> Chief Judge Royce Lamberth, USDC,
> District of Columbia

The discovery violations described above and in Chapter 3 are egregious but not malicious. But in some cases, discovery misconduct can be downright nefarious. There are instances of witnesses being hidden or not provided, documents being deliberately withheld or destroyed, illegal wiretapping and even dumpster diving for privileged evidence.

There are a discouraging number of severe benchslaps to choose from for dishonest and often unlawful discovery misconduct. However, none trumps the staggering benchslap issued by Magistrate Judge Barbara Major in the Southern District of California in *Qualcomm v. Broadcom*. In this lengthy excerpt from an even lengthier 42-page opinion, Judge Major calls out each member of the "Qualcomm Six" by name, and provides an attachment detailing their professional history and the role they played in the misconduct.

… As summarized above, and as found by Judge Brewster, there is clear and convincing evidence that Qualcomm intentionally engaged in conduct designed to prevent Broadcom from learning that Qualcomm had participated in the JVT during the time period when the H.264 standard was being developed. To this end, Qualcomm withheld tens of thousands of emails showing that it actively participated in the JVT in 2002 and 2003 and then utilized Broadcom's lack of access to the suppressed evidence to repeatedly and falsely aver that there was "no evidence" that it had participated in the JVT prior to September 2003. Qualcomm's misconduct in hiding the emails and electronic documents prevented Broadcom from correcting the false statements and countering the misleading arguments. . .

As summarized above, Broadcom served interrogatories and requested documents relating to Qualcomm's participation in the JVT. Qualcomm responded that "Qualcomm will produce non-privileged relevant and responsive documents describing QUALCOMM's participation in the JVT, if any, which can be located after a reasonable search." Doc. No. 543-3, Ex. X (Qualcomm's Response to Broadcom's Request for

Production No. 93). Qualcomm also committed to producing "responsive non-privileged documents that were given to or received from standards-setting body responsible for the [H.264] standard, and which concern any Qualcomm participation in setting the [H.264] standard." Mammen Decl. at 7-8.

> "Qualcomm did not produce over 46,000 responsive documents, many of which directly contradict the ... argument [it] repeatedly made to the court and jury."

Despite these responses, Qualcomm did not produce over 46,000 responsive documents, many of which directly contradict the nonparticipation argument that Qualcomm repeatedly made to the court and jury. Because Qualcomm agreed to produce the documents and answered the interrogatories (even though falsely), Broadcom had no reason to file a motion to compel. And, because Broadcom did not file a motion to compel, Broadcom's possible remedies are restricted. If Broadcom had filed a motion to compel, it could have obtained sanctions against Qualcomm and its attorneys. Fed. R. Civ. P. 37(a) & (b). Because Broadcom did not file a motion to compel, it may only seek Rule 37 sanctions against Qualcomm. Fed. R. Civ. P. 37(c). Thus, Qualcomm's suppression of documents placed its retained attorneys in a better legal position than they would have been in if Qualcomm had refused to produce the documents and Broadcom had filed a motion to compel.

This dilemma highlights another problem with Qualcomm's conduct in this case. The Federal Rules of Civil Procedure require parties to respond to discovery in good faith;

the rules do not require or anticipate judicial involvement unless or until an actual dispute is discovered. As the Advisory Committee explained, "[i]f primary responsibility for conducting discovery is to continue to rest with the litigants, they must be obliged to act responsibly and avoid abuse." Fed. R. Civ. P. 26(g) Advisory Committee Notes (1983 Amendment). The Committee's concerns are heightened in this age of electronic discovery when attorneys may not physically touch and read every document within the client's custody and control. For the current "good faith" discovery system to function in the electronic age, attorneys and clients must work together to ensure that both understand how and where electronic documents, records and emails are maintained and to determine how best to locate, review, and produce responsive documents. Attorneys must take responsibility for ensuring that their clients conduct a comprehensive and appropriate document search. Producing 1.2 million pages of marginally relevant documents while hiding 46,000 critically important ones does not constitute good faith and does not satisfy either the client's or attorney's discovery obligations. Similarly, agreeing to produce certain categories of documents and then not producing all of the documents that fit within such a category is unacceptable. Qualcomm's conduct warrants sanctions.

> "Producing 1.2 million pages of marginally relevant documents while hiding 46,000 critically important ones does not constitute good faith."

The Court's review of Qualcomm's declarations, the attorneys' declarations, and Judge Brewster's orders leads this Court to the inevitable conclusion that Qualcomm intentionally withheld tens of thousands of decisive documents from its opponent in an effort to win this case and gain a strategic business advantage over Broadcom. Qualcomm could not have achieved this goal without some type of assistance or deliberate ignorance from its retained attorneys. Accordingly, the Court concludes it must sanction both Qualcomm and some of its retained attorneys.

Qualcomm violated its discovery obligations by failing to produce more than 46,000 emails and documents that were requested in discovery and that Qualcomm agreed to produce. See Fed. R. Civ. P. 26(g) Advisory Committee Notes (1983 Amendment) ("Rule 26(g) imposes an affirmative duty to engage in pretrial discovery in a responsible manner that is consistent with the spirit and purposes of Rules 26 through 37). Rule 37 dictates that "[a] party that without substantial justification fails to ... amend a prior response to discovery as required by Rule 26(e)(2), is not, unless such failure is harmless, permitted to use" the suppressed evidence in court proceedings. Fed. R. Civ. P. 37(c)(1). The court also may impose other appropriate sanctions, including the imposition of reasonable attorneys' fees. Id.

Qualcomm has not established "substantial justification" for its failure to produce the documents. In fact, Qualcomm has not presented *any* evidence attempting to explain or justify its failure to produce the documents. Despite the fact that it maintains detailed records showing whose computers were searched and which search terms were used (Glathe Decl. at 3 (identifying the individuals whose computers were not searched for specific types of documents)), Qualcomm has not presented any evidence establishing that it searched for pre-

September 2003 JVT, avc_ce, or H.264 records or emails on its computer system or email databases. Qualcomm also has not established that it searched the computers or email databases of the individuals who testified on Qualcomm's behalf at trial or in depositions as Qualcomm's most knowledgeable corporate witnesses; in fact, it indicates that it did not conduct any such search. *Id.*; Irvine Decl. at 2; Ludwin Decl. at 3; Decl. of Viji Raveendran at 1, 4. The fact that Qualcomm did not perform these basic searches at any time before the completion of trial indicates that Qualcomm intentionally withheld the documents. This conclusion is bolstered by the fact that when Qualcomm "discovered" the 21 Raveendran emails, it did not produce them and did not engage in any type of review to determine whether there were additional relevant, responsive, and unproduced documents. Bier Decl. at 7; Mammen Decl. at 16-18; Patch Decl. at 5-7. The conclusion is further supported by the fact that after trial Qualcomm did not conduct an internal investigation to determine if there were additional unproduced documents (Bier Decl., Ex. E (Qualcomm still had not searched as of March 7, 2007)); but, rather, spent its time opposing Broadcom's efforts to force such a search and insisting, without any factual basis, that Qualcomm's search was reasonable. *Id.* at 10-11, Exs. B-F; Patch Decl. at 11-14.

Qualcomm's claim that it inadvertently failed to find and produce these documents also is negated by the massive volume and direct relevance of the hidden documents. As Judge Brewster noted, it is inexplicable that Qualcomm was able to locate the post-September 2003 JVT documents that either supported, or did not harm, Qualcomm's arguments but were unable to locate the pre-September 2003 JVT documents that hurt its arguments. Waiver Order at 38. Similarly, the inadvertence argument is undercut by Qualcomm's ability to easily locate the suppressed documents using fundamental JVT and avc search terms when forced to do so by Broadcom's threat to return to court. See October 12, 2007 Hearing Transcript at 192. Finally, the inadvertence argument also is belied by the number of Qualcomm employees and consultants who received the emails, attended the JVT meetings, and otherwise knew about the information set forth in the undisclosed emails. Waiver Order at 10-12, 21-32. It is inconceivable that Qualcomm was unaware of its involvement in the JVT and of the existence of these documents. . .

Qualcomm had the ability to identify its employees and consultants who were involved in the JVT, to access and review their computers, databases and emails, to talk with the involved employees and to refresh their recollections if necessary, to ensure that those testifying about the corporation's knowledge were sufficiently prepared and testified accurately, and to produce in good faith all relevant and requested discovery. *See Nat'l Assoc. of Radiation Survivors v. Turnage*, 115 F.R.D. 543, 557-58 (N.D. Cal. 1987) (holding in case where sanctions imposed for withholding of documents that "a reasonable inquiry into the factual basis of its discovery responses as well as the factual basis of subsequent pleadings, papers, and motions based on those responses . . . would have required, at a minimum, a reasonable procedure to distribute discovery requests to all employees and agents of the defendant potentially possessing responsive information, and to account for the collection and subsequent production of the information"). Qualcomm chose not to do so and therefore must be sanctioned.

The next question is what, if any, role did Qualcomm's retained lawyers play in withholding the documents? The Court envisions four scenarios. First, Qualcomm intentionally hid the documents from its retained lawyers and did so so effectively that the lawyers did not know or suspect that the suppressed documents existed. Second, the retained lawyers failed to discover the intentionally hidden documents or suspect their existence due to their complete ineptitude and disorganization. Third, Qualcomm shared the damaging documents with its retained lawyers (or at least some of them) and the knowledgeable lawyers worked with Qualcomm to hide the documents and all evidence of Qualcomm's early involvement in the JVT. Or, fourth, while Qualcomm did not tell the retained lawyers about the damaging documents and evidence, the lawyers suspected there was additional evidence or information but chose to ignore the evidence and warning signs and accept Qualcomm's incredible assertions regarding the adequacy of the document search and witness investigation.

Given the impressive education and extensive experience of Qualcomm's retained lawyers (see exhibit A7), the Court rejects the first and second possibilities. It is inconceivable that these talented, well-educated, and experienced lawyers failed to discover through their interactions with Qualcomm any facts or issues that caused (or should have caused) them to question the sufficiency of Qualcomm's document search and

"It is inconceivable that these talented, well-educated, and experienced lawyers failed to discover … any facts or issues that caused (or should have caused) them to question the sufficiency of Qualcomm's document search and production."

production. Qualcomm did not fail to produce a document or two; it withheld over 46,000 critical documents that extinguished Qualcomm's primary argument of non-participation in the JVT. In addition, the suppressed documents did not belong to one employee, or a couple of employees who had since left the company; they belonged to (or were shared with) numerous, current Qualcomm employees, several of whom testified (falsely) at trial and in depositions. Given the volume and importance of the withheld documents, the number of involved Qualcomm employees, and the numerous warning flags, the Court finds it unbelievable that the retained attorneys did not know or suspect that Qualcomm had not conducted an adequate search for documents.

The Court finds no direct evidence establishing option three. Neither party nor the attorneys have presented evidence that Qualcomm told one or more of its retained attorneys about the damaging emails or that an attorney learned about the emails and that the knowledgeable attorney(s) then helped Qualcomm hide the emails. While knowledge may be inferred from the attorneys' conduct, evidence on this issue is limited due to Qualcomm's assertion of the attorney-client privilege.

> "[Counsels'] choices enabled Qualcomm to withhold hundreds of thousands of pages of relevant discovery and to assert numerous false and misleading arguments."

Thus, the Court finds it likely that some variation of option four occurred; that is, one or more of the retained lawyers chose not to look in the correct locations for the correct documents, to accept the unsubstantiated assurances of an important client that its search was sufficient, to ignore the warning signs that the document search and production were inadequate, not to press Qualcomm employees for the truth, and/or to encourage employees to provide the information (or lack of information) that Qualcomm needed to assert its non-participation argument and to succeed in this lawsuit. These choices enabled Qualcomm to withhold hundreds of thousands of pages of relevant discovery and to assert numerous false and misleading arguments to the court and jury. This conduct warrants the imposition of sanctions.

The Court finds that each of the following attorneys contributed to Qualcomm's monumental discovery violation and is personally responsible: James Batchelder, Adam Bier, Kevin Leung, Christopher Mammen, Lee Patch, and Stanley Young ("Sanctioned Attorneys").

Attorneys Leung, Mammen and Batchelder are responsible for the initial discovery failure because they handled or supervised Qualcomm's discovery responses and production of documents. The Federal Rules impose an affirmative duty upon lawyers to engage in discovery in a responsible manner and to conduct a "reasonable inquiry" to determine whether discovery responses are sufficient and proper. Fed. R. Civ. P. 26(g); Fed. R. Civ. P. 26 Advisory Committee Notes (1983 Amendment). In the instant case, a reasonable inquiry should have included searches using fundamental terms such as JVT, avc_ce or H.264, on the computers belonging to knowledgeable people such as Raveendran, Irvine and Ludwin. As the post-trial investigation confirmed, such a reasonable search would have revealed the suppressed documents. Had Leung, Mammen, Batchelder, or any of the other attorneys insisted on reviewing Qualcomm's records regarding the locations searched and terms utilized, they would have discovered the inadequacy of the search and the suppressed documents. Similarly, Leung's difficulties with the Rule 30(b)(6) witnesses, Irvine and Ludwin, should have alerted him (and the supervising or senior attorneys) to the inadequacy of Qualcomm's document production and to the fact that they needed to review whose computers and databases had been searched and for what. Accordingly, the Court finds that the totality of the circumstances establish that Leung, Mammen and Batchelder did not make a reasonable inquiry into Qualcomm's discovery search and production and their conduct contributed to the discovery violation.

Attorneys Bier, Mammen and Patch are responsible for the discovery violation because they also did not perform a reasonable inquiry to determine whether Qualcomm had complied with its discovery obligations. When Bier reviewed the August 6, 2002 email welcoming Raveendran to the avc_ce email group, he knew or should have known that it contradicted Qualcomm's trial arguments and he had an obligation to verify that it had been produced in discovery or to immediately produce it. If Bier, as a junior lawyer, lacked the experience to recognize the significance of the document, then a more senior or knowledgeable attorney should have assisted him. To the extent that Patch was supervising Bier in this endeavor, Patch certainly knew or should have recognized the importance of the document from his involvement in Qualcomm's motion practice and trial strategy sessions.

Similarly, when Bier found the 21 emails on Raveendran's computer that had not been produced in discovery, he took the appropriate action and informed his supervisors, Mammen and Patch. Bier Decl. at 7. Patch discussed the discovery and production issue with Young and Batchelder. Patch Decl. at 6-7. While all of these attorneys assert that there was a plausible argument that Broadcom did not request these documents, only Bier and Mammen actually read the emails. Patch Decl. at 6-7; Batchelder Decl. at 16. Moreover, all of the attorneys missed the critical inquiry: was Qualcomm's document search adequate? If these 21 emails were not discovered during Qualcomm's document search, how many more might exist? The answer, obviously, was tens of thousands. If Bier, Mammen, Patch, Young or Batchelder had conducted a reasonable inquiry after the discovery of the 21 Raveendran emails, they would have discovered the inadequacy of Qualcomm's search and the suppressed documents. And, these experienced attorneys should have realized that the presence on Raveendran's computer of 21 JVT/avc_ce emails from 2002 contradicted Qualcomm's numerous arguments that it had not participated in the JVT during that same time period. This fact, alone, should have prompted the attorneys to immediately produce the emails and to conduct a comprehensive document search.

Finally, attorneys Young, Patch, and Batchelder bear responsibility for the discovery failure because they did not conduct a reasonable inquiry into Qualcomm's discovery production before making specific factual and legal arguments to the court. Young decided that Qualcomm should file a motion for summary adjudication premised on the fact that Qualcomm had not participated in the JVT until after the H.264 standard was adopted in May 2003. Given that non-participation was vital to the motion, Young had a duty to conduct a reasonable inquiry into whether that fact was true. And, again, had Young conducted such a search, he would have discovered the inadequacy of Qualcomm's document search and production and learned that his argument was false. Similarly, Young had a duty to conduct a reasonable inquiry into the accuracy of his statement before affirmatively telling the court that no emails were sent to Raveendran from the avc_ce email group. Young also did not conduct a reasonable (or any) inquiry during the following days before he approved the factually incorrect JMOL. A reasonable investigation would have prevented the false filing.

Patch was an integral part of the trial team-familiar with Qualcomm's arguments, theories and strategies. He knew on January 1Fourth that 21 avc_ce emails had been discovered on Raveendran's computer. Without reading or reviewing the emails, Patch participated in the decision not to produce them. Several days later, Patch carefully tailored his questions to ensure that Raveendran did not testify about the unproduced emails. And, after Broadcom stumbled into the email testimony, Patch affirmatively misled the Court by claiming that he did not know whether the emails were responsive to Broadcom's discovery requests. This conduct is unacceptable and, considering the totality of the circumstances, it is unrealistic to think that Patch did not know or believe that Qualcomm's document search was inadequate and that Qualcomm possessed numerous, similar and unproduced documents.

Batchelder also is responsible because he was the lead trial attorney and, as such, he was most familiar with Qualcomm's important arguments and witnesses. Batchelder stated in his opening statement that Qualcomm had not participated in the JVT before late 2003. Despite this statement and his complete knowledge of Qualcomm's legal theories, Batchelder did not take any action when he was informed that JVT documents that Qualcomm had not produced in discovery were found on Raveendran's computer. He did not read the emails, ask about their substance, nor inquire as to why they were not located during discovery. And, he stood mute when four days later, Young falsely stated that no emails had been sent to Raveendran from the avc_ce email group. Finally, all of the pleadings containing the lie that Qualcomm had not participated in the JVT in 2002 or early 2003 were sent to Batchelder for review and he approved or ignored all of them. The totality of the circumstances, including all of the previously-discussed warning signs, demanded that Batchelder conduct an investigation to verify the adequacy of Qualcomm's document search and production. His failure to do so enabled Qualcomm to withhold the documents.

For all of these reasons, the Court finds that these attorneys did not conduct a reasonable inquiry into the adequacy of Qualcomm's document search and production and, accordingly, they are responsible, along with Qualcomm, for the monumental discovery violation.

Based upon the Court's review of the submitted declarations (see Exhibit A), the Court finds that the following attorneys do not bear any individual responsibility for the discovery violation and, on that basis, declines to sanction them: Ruchika Agrawal, Howard Loo, William Nelson, Ryan Scher, Bradley Waugh, David Kleinfeld, Barry Tucker, Heidi

Gutierrez, Victoria Smith, Roy Zemlicka, Craig Casebeer, Jaideep Venkatesan, and Kyle Robertson.

The Court declines to sanction attorneys Agrawal, Loo, Nelson, Scher, Waugh and Guiterrez because they did not significantly participate in the preparation or prosecution of the instant case or primarily participated in aspects of the case unrelated to those at issue in this Order and Judge Brewster's Waiver Order and Exceptional Case Order. See Exhibit A.

The Court also declines to sanction Heller Ehrman attorneys Kleinfeld and Tucker. These attorneys primarily monitored the instant case for its impact on separate Qualcomm/Broadcom litigation. However, for logistical reasons, both attorneys signed as local counsel pleadings that contained false statements relating to Qulacomm's non-participation in the JVT. Given the facts of this case as set forth above and in the declarations, the limitations provided by the referral, and the totality of the circumstances, the Court finds that it was reasonable for these attorneys to sign the pleadings, relying on the work of other attorneys more actively involved in the litigation.

While a closer call, the Court also declines to sanction Day Casebeer attorneys Casebeer, Smith and Zemlicka. Unlike the Sanctioned Attorneys, Casebeer did not begin working on this case until after discovery had closed and he did not learn about the Raveendran emails until after she testified at trial. Thus, he would not have been privy to any of the red flags, which should have alerted the Sanctioned Attorneys to the fact that significant discovery gaps existed and further investigation was necessary.

Smith and Zemlicka prepared and signed pleadings containing false statements about Qualcomm's non-participation in the JVT. While they did more substantive work on the false motions than Kleinfeld and Tucker, all four relied on work conducted by other lawyers who were more involved in the discovery and litigation. In addition, Smith and Zemlicka worked under the direction of Casebeer who told them to rely on and conform the motion to the discussion of facts set forth in Qualcomm's MSA. Although the Court questions the reasonableness of the attorneys' decision to rely on the MSA without conducting any independent investigation under the facts of this case, the Court concludes that the totality of the circumstances do not justify sanctioning Zemlicka or Smith. This conclusion is bolstered by the fact that the pleadings were reviewed and approved by attorneys with more litigation experience and more familiarity with this case.

For similar reasons, the Court finds it inappropriate to individually sanction Heller Ehrman attorneys Kyle Robertson and Jaideep Venkatesan. These attorneys, working for Stanley Young, began work on JVT-related issues in August 2006. Robertson, under the supervision of Venkatesan, made significant efforts to confirm the accuracy of the facts upon which he relied in drafting various pleadings, including:

(1) reviewing numerous deposition transcripts and discovery responses,

(2) circulating drafts of all pleadings he prepared to more senior outside and inside counsel with the expectation

that they would inform him of any factual inaccuracies, and

(3) upon learning from Broadcom's opposition to the MSA of the December 2002 report listing Raveendran's email address, searching the JVT website for information about the Ad- Hoc Group email list, contacting numerous Day Casebeer and Heller Ehrman attorneys for more information, and finally calling Raveendran at home.

The Court again finds it troubling that these attorneys failed to investigate the adequacy of Qualcomm's document search and production before filing the pleadings but, given the totality of the circumstances, the Court declines to sanction Robertson and Venkatesan.

As set forth above, the evidence establishes that Qualcomm intentionally withheld tens of thousands of emails and that the Sanctioned Attorneys assisted, either intentionally or by virtue of acting with reckless disregard for their discovery obligations, in this discovery violation. The remaining issue, then, is what are the appropriate sanctions...

Monetary sanctions . . . are appropriate. The suppressed emails directly rebutted Qualcomm's argument that it had not participated in the JVT during the time the H.264 standard was being developed. As such, their absence was critical to Qualcomm's hope and intent of enforcing its patents against Broadcom (as well as presumably all other cellular companies utilizing the H.264 technology in their products). Because Broadcom prevailed at trial and in the post-trial hearings despite the suppressed evidence, it is reasonable to infer that had Qualcomm intended to produce the 46,000 incriminating emails (and thereby acknowledge its early involvement in the JVT and its accompanying need to disclose its intellectual property), the instant case may never have been filed.16 Even if Qualcomm did file this case, the hidden evidence would have dramatically undermined Qualcomm's arguments and likely resulted in an adverse pretrial adjudication, much as it caused the adverse post-trial rulings. See Waiver Order; Exceptional Case Order. Accordingly, Qualcomm's failure to produce the massive number of critical documents at issue in this case significantly increased the scope, complexity and length of the litigation and justifies a significant monetary award. See, Fed. R. Civ. P. 26(g)(3) & 37(c).

The Court therefore awards Broadcom all of its attorneys' fees and costs incurred in the instant litigation. Because Judge Brewster already has awarded these costs and fees to Broadcom in the Exceptional Case Order and a double recovery would be improper, this Court directs that Qualcomm receive credit toward this penalty for any money it pays to Broadcom to satisfy the exceptional case award. Accordingly, for its monumental and intentional discovery violation, Qualcomm is ordered to pay $8,568,633.24 to Broadcom; this figure will be reduced by the amount actually paid by Qualcomm to Broadcom to satisfy the exceptional case award.

As set forth above, the Sanctioned Attorneys assisted Qualcomm in committing this incredible discovery violation by intentionally hiding or recklessly ignoring relevant documents, ignoring or rejecting numerous warning signs that Qualcomm's document search was inadequate, and blindly accepting

Qualcomm's unsupported assurances that its document search was adequate. The Sanctioned Attorneys then used the lack of evidence to repeatedly and forcefully make false statements and arguments to the court and jury. As such, the Sanctioned Attorneys violated their discovery obligations and also may have violated their ethical duties. See e.g., The State Bar of California, Rules of Professional Conduct, Rule 5-200 (a lawyer shall not seek to mislead the judge or jury by a false statement of fact or law), Rule 5-220 (a lawyer shall not suppress evidence that the lawyer or the lawyer's client has a legal obligation to reveal or to produce). To address the potential ethical violations, the Court refers the Sanctioned Attorneys to The State Bar of California for an appropriate investigation and possible imposition of sanctions. Within ten days of the date of this Order, each of the Sanctioned Attorneys must forward a copy of this Order and Judge Brewster's Waiver Order to the Intake Unit, The State Bar of California, 1149 South Hill Street, Los Angeles, California 90015 for appropriate investigation.

The Court also orders Qualcomm and the Sanctioned Attorneys to participate in a comprehensive Case Review and Enforcement of Discovery Obligations ("CREDO") program. This is a collaborative process to identify the failures in the case management and discovery protocol utilized by Qualcomm and its in-house and retained attorneys in this case, to craft alternatives that will prevent such failures in the future, to evaluate and test the alternatives, and ultimately, to create a case management protocol which will serve as a model for the future.

Because they reviewed and approved the false pleadings, the Court designates the following Qualcomm attorneys to participate in this process as Qualcomm's representatives: Alex Rogers, Roger Martin, William Sailer, Byron Yafuso, and Michael Hartogs (the "Named Qualcomm Attorneys"). Qualcomm employees were integral participants in hiding documents and making false statements to the court and jury. Qualcomm's in-house lawyers were in the unique position of (a) having unlimited access to all Qualcomm employees, as well as the emails and documents maintained, possessed and used by them, (b) knowing or being able to determine all of the computers and databases that were searched and the search terms that were utilized, and (c) having the ability to review all of the pleadings filed on Qualcomm's behalf which did (or should have) alerted them to the fact that either the document search was inadequate or they were knowingly not producing tens of thousands of relevant and requested documents. Accordingly, Qualcomm's in-house lawyers need to be involved in this process.

At a minimum, the CREDO protocol must include a detailed analysis (1) identifying the factors 20 that contributed to the discovery violation (e.g., insufficient communication (including between client and retained counsel, among retained lawyers and law firms, and between junior lawyers conducting discovery and senior lawyers asserting legal arguments); inadequate case management (within Qualcomm, between Qualcomm and the retained lawyers, and by the retained lawyers); inadequate discovery plans (within Qualcomm and between Qualcomm and its retained attorneys); etc.), (2) creating and evaluating proposals, procedures, and processes that will correct the deficiencies identified in subsection (1), (3) developing and finalizing a comprehensive protocol that will prevent future discovery violations (e.g., determining the depth and breadth of case management and discovery plans that should be adopted; identifying by experience or authority the attorney from the retained counsel's office who should interface with the corporate counsel and on which issues; describing the frequency the attorneys should meet and whether other individuals should participate in the communications; identifying who should participate in the development of the case management and discovery plans; describing and evaluating various methods of resolving conflicts and disputes between the client and retained counsel, especially relating to the adequacy of discovery searches; describing the type, nature, frequency, and participants in case management and discovery meetings; and, suggesting required ethical and discovery training; etc.), (4) applying the protocol that was developed in subsection (3) to other factual situations, such as when the client does not have corporate counsel, when the client has a single in-house lawyer, when the client has a large legal staff, and when there are two law firms representing one client, (5) identifying and evaluating data tracking systems, software, or procedures that corporations could implement to better enable inside and outside counsel to identify potential sources of discoverable documents (e.g. the correct databases, archives, etc.), and (6) any other information or suggestions that will help prevent discovery violations.

To facilitate development of the CREDO program, the Sanctioned Attorneys and Named Qualcomm Attorneys are required to meet21 at 9:00 a.m. on Tuesday, January 29, 2008, in the chambers of the Honorable Barbara L. Major, United States Magistrate Judge, 940 Front Street, Suite 5140, San Diego, California, 92101. The Court will participate only to the extent necessary to ensure that the participants are complying with the instructions in this Order. The Court will provide whatever time is necessary for the participants to fully and completely examine, analyze and complete the CREDO protocol. At the conclusion of the process, the participating attorneys will submit their proposed protocol to the Court. The Court will review the proposed protocol and, if sufficient, order it filed. The Court will notify the Sanctioned Attorneys and Named Qualcomm Attorneys if the proposed protocol is insufficient so further revisions can be implemented. When completed protocol is submitted, the Sanctioned Attorneys and Named Qualcomm Attorneys shall each file a declaration under penalty of perjury affirming that they personally participated in the entire process that led to the CREDO protocol and specifying the amount of time they spent working on it.

While no one can undo the misconduct in this case, this process, hopefully, will establish a baseline for other cases. Perhaps it also will establish a turning point in what the Court perceives as a decline in and deterioration of civility, professionalism and ethical conduct in the litigation arena. To the extent it does so, everyone benefits - Broadcom, Qualcomm, and all attorneys who engage in, and judges who preside over, complex litigation. If nothing else, it will provide a road map to assist counsel and corporate clients in complying with their ethical and discovery obligations and conducting the requisite "reasonable inquiry."

Magistrate Judge Barbara Major, USDC,
Central District of California

The story of the "Qualcomm Six" has an interesting and unfortunate postscript. Shortly after Judge Major's staggering benchslap, the attorneys involved appealed their sanctions to the trial court judge, who removed the sanctions and ordered Judge Major to reconsider sanctions after hearing argument from counsel. Nearly two years after sanctions were originally imposed, that same Judge Major reversed course and declined to re-issue sanctions:

On January 7, 2008, this Court issued an Order Granting in Part and Denying in Part Defendant's Motion for Sanctions and Sanctioning Qualcomm Incorporated and Individual Lawyers ("Sanctions Order"). Doc. No. 718. The Court found that Plaintiff Qualcomm Incorporated ("Qualcomm") intentionally withheld tens of thousands of documents that Defendant Broadcom Corporation ("Broadcom") had requested in discovery. . .

The Court specifically identified several inadequacies in Qualcomm's document search that should have been apparent to outside counsel, including the failure to search the computers belonging to, or used by, deponents and trial witnesses, the failure to adequately investigate when significant, relevant, and unproduced documents were discovered, and the failure to ensure there was a legitimate factual basis for the legal arguments made to the Court before making them. Qualcomm did not appeal the $8.5 million sanction imposed against it.

The sanctioned attorneys ("Responding Attorneys") filed objections to the Sanctions Order with the trial judge, United States District Judge Rudi M. Brewster. On March 5, 2008, Judge Brewster vacated the Sanctions Order as to the Responding Attorneys and remanded the matter to this Court, finding that the Responding Attorneys had a due process right to defend themselves and, therefore, should "not be prevented from defending their conduct by the attorney-client privilege of Qualcomm and its employees and representatives because of the application of the self-defense exception to the attorney-client privilege of Qualcomm." …

There still is no doubt in this Court's mind that this massive discovery failure resulted from significant mistakes, oversights, and miscommunication on the part of both outside counsel and Qualcomm employees. The new facts and evidence presented to this Court during the remand proceedings revealed ineffective and problematic interactions between Qualcomm employees and most of the Responding Attorneys during the pretrial litigation, including the commission of a number of critical errors. However, it also revealed that the Responding Attorneys made significant efforts to comply with their discovery obligations. After considering all of the new facts, the Court declines to sanction any of the Responding Attorneys…

> "After considering all of the new facts, the Court declines to sanction any of the Responding attorneys."

The evidence presented during these proceedings clarified that, although a number of poor decisions were made, the involved attorneys did not act in bad faith. While Leung and

Mammen did not pursue several discovery paths that seem obvious, at least in hindsight, they did make repeated efforts to verify that Qualcomm's discovery responses were accurate. Similarly, when Patch became involved in discovery, while he did not determine whether Raveendran's personal computer had been searched, he did take numerous, reasonable steps to verify the truth of her statements...

In summary, while the Court believes the attorneys should have considered the contents of the documents and their relevance to the arguments being presented in court and to the adequacy of the discovery process, the Court finds that the evidence does not establish that any of the Responding Attorneys acted in bad faith...

> "[T]he evidence does not establish that any of the Responding attorneys acted in bad faith."

It is undisputed that Qualcomm improperly withheld from Broadcom tens of thousands of documents that contradicted one of its key legal arguments. However, the evidence presented during these remand proceedings has established that while significant errors were made by some of the Responding Attorneys, there is insufficient evidence to prove that any of the Responding Attorneys engaged in the requisite "bad faith" or that Leung failed to make a reasonable inquiry before certifying Qualcomm's discovery responses. Accordingly, the Court declines to impose sanctions on the Responding Attorneys and hereby dissolves the order to show cause that initiated these proceedings.[54]

Magistrate Judge Barbara Major, USDC,
Central District of California

———————————

While the "Qualcomm Six" may be legally vindicated, that vindication does nothing to repair the harm they suffered in their personal and professional lives as a result of their public shaming. Many attorneys are familiar with the "Qualcomm Six" opinion; very few are aware those attorneys were later exonerated. In an era of Google, blogs and electronic background checks, Judge Major's benchslap will follow each of the "Qualcomm Six" throughout their careers. Her subsequent decision not to re-issue sanctions does little to change that.

Attorney Adam Bier, who was just a fourth-year associate at the time he was sanctioned as one of the "Qualcomm Six," left his big firm job shortly after being sanctioned and was untouchable by legal recruiters as a result of the Qualcomm sanctions.[55] With few career options, Mr. Bier, an NYU law grad with patent experience, took a fellowship at a renewable energy non-profit and began stocking up on CLE credits. In April 2009, he opened his own firm, where he was able to avoid the specter of the Qualcomm sanctions.

Three of the other "Qualcomm Six" – Kevin Leung, Chris Mamen and Lee Patch – spoke to the ABA Journal about their experience shortly after Judge Major's order declining to re-issue sanctions.[56] All three left their firm under "strained circumstances" and were unable to find new employment at large firms. As of mid-2010, Mr. Leung was doing patent work for a friend's firm, Mr. Mammen was teaching part-time at the

Hastings College of Law and Mr. Patch was working as an independent consultant. In his interview with the ABA Journal, Mr. Leung lamented that Judge Major's benchslap "really derailed my path through life and kind of put me on ice." Mr. Patch noted that the opinion and its aftermath made him worry whether he could support his 13-year old twins. "This kind of thing can happen to anybody," he said.

The serious consequences of public benchslaps in the digital age should give judges pause. Given that such opinions may be retracted but not forgotten, one wonders whether a publicly humiliating judicial opinion is ever appropriate, even when seemingly deserved.

CHAPTER 5: Rules Rebukes

It should come as no surprise that judges love rules. They read rules, interpret rules and enforce rules. Inside their courtrooms, they make the rules. Statutes and case law have granted judges broad discretion to implement and enforce procedural rules in their courtrooms and they do so to the fullest extent. But their reasons for doing so may go beyond a simple love of laws.

Absent strong procedural rules, judges would be buried by ever-increasing workloads. In 1997, approximately 270,000 civil cases and 50,000 criminal cases were filed in the 94 federal district courts.[57] By 2010, there were more than 300,000 civil cases pending and 77,000 criminal cases.[58] During this same period, the number of active district court judges declined and resources for district courts dwindled even as cases, especially those involving detailed or voluminous discovery, became more complicated and time-intensive. In California, the state court budget has been reduced by hundreds of millions of dollars over the past three years.[59] More cuts are on the table in California and the same is true across nearly all states. Judges must rely on strict procedural rules to streamline case management and ensure they can give appropriate attention to the thousands of filings they review and rule on each year.

Another and more cynical explanation for judges' adherence to strict procedural rules is that such rules allow judges to bump cases without reviewing the merits. If a difficult brief is ten-percent too long, a judge can disregard it. If a pleading is one-hour late, it can be similarly ignored. While some judges shy away from remedies that prejudice a client for an attorney's error, others have no qualms about ignoring pleadings or dismissing cases for procedural violations. When Harvard law professor Charles Nesson sought to file an *amicus* brief in a civil proceeding, it was disregarded with only the following cursory note from U.S. District Court Judge Michael Davis, which was issued the same day the brief was filed:

> On November 1, Professor Charles Nesson filed an unsolicited brief entitled "Amicus Curiae Brief on the Issue of Jury Instructions. [Docket No. 403] Nesson is not a party to this action; nor does he represent any party in this action. Nesson has not asked for permission to intervene or to file and amicus brief. Moreover, he has filed a brief regarding a jury instruction issue that was already fully briefed, argued, and decided more than one week ago.[60]

Readers may be happy to note that even Harvard law professors get benchslapped sometimes. (Mr. Nesson learned from his mistake and later sought permission from the court before filing further *amicus* briefs.)

Even when the consequences of rules violations are not catastrophic, they are intensely embarrassing. This is partly because compliance with court rules is among the few things over which an attorney has complete control. Such rules are easily accessible and rarely onerous, making it hard to justify good faith misunderstandings or lack of knowledge. For this reason, discipline for rules violations can be heavy-handed, even for minor infractions. Consider the following case involving the prestigious international firm Morrison & Forester, in which a brief that arrived at the courtroom just a few minutes late cost the firm's client millions of dollars:

> The 14 day deadline under Rule 54(d)(2)(B) includes Saturdays, Sundays, and legal holidays. Failure to file a motion to attorneys' fees within the prescribed time period waives a party's right to request fees. [Citation omitted]. Fed. R. Civ. Proc. 6(b), however, permits a court to enlarge the period of time within which a party must file a motion for attorneys' fees "where the failure to act was the result of excusable neglect…" Unfortunately for TAIS, its one day delay in filing its motion was not the result of "excusable neglect."…

> Here, TAIS' purported reason for its delay is that its courier was caught in traffic at 3:30 in the afternoon in Santa Ana, California. Mr. Mersel, attorney for TAIS, asserts that he waited until 3:14 p.m. on the last day of the filing period to deliver the motion to Morrisson & Foerster's regular courier service. (Mersel Decl., ¶ 2.) Mr. Mersel asserts that although he was aware that the filing deadline was 4:00 p.m., he had "never

had a problem with getting papers filed by 4:00 p.m. when delivering them to the attorney service" forty-five minutes in advance. (*Id.*) The courier, Mr. Moskus, swiftly responded to Mr. Mersel's request, leaving on his motorcycle for the courthouse at approximately 3:30 p.m. (Moskus Decl., ¶ 3.) Unfortunately, Mr. Moskus encountered "unusually heavy traffic" and had to "wait at the railroad crossing on Grand Avenue for a long train to pass."(Moskus Decl., ¶ 3.) Consequently, Mr. Moskus arrived at the Courthouse after the office had closed and Mr. Mersel was unable to file the motion until the following day, on October 11, 2007. (Mersel Decl., ¶ 7.)

These circumstances, however regrettable, do not meet the standard for "excusable neglect." Although the delay was not lengthy and it does not appear that NETI was prejudiced by it, the reason for the delay was entirely with TAIS' control and TAIS has not offered a good faith reason for the delay. Given that the Ninth Circuit has held that a good faith misunderstanding of local rules is not sufficient to rise to the standard of "excusable neglect," the entirely foreseeable obstacle of traffic in Southern California in the late afternoon also cannot justify an enlargement of time. Unlike the parties in *Yost* and *Kyle*, Mr. Mersel is not even arguing that he had a good faith reason to believe that he had extra time to file the motion for fees. Instead, Mr. Mersel asserts that he has a practice of waiting until 45 minutes prior to the filing deadline before passing off a motion to his courier, and because

> "[T]he entirely foreseeable obstacle of traffic in Southern California in the late afternoon also cannot justify an enlargement of time."

that plan has worked in the past, it should have been sufficient on this occasion. Although this pattern of conduct may have previously worked for Mr. Mersel, it is not a good faith reason for the delay. Unlike the circumstances discussed in *Yost* that would constitute legitimate reasons for the delay, such as the illness of counsel or destruction of his law office, the reason for delay in this case was entirely foreseeable and avoidable. Mr. Mersel knew since at least September 10, 2007, the date of this Court's Tentative Order … that he would need to prepare a motion for attorney's fees. He waited a month later, until 3:14 p.m. on October 10, to attempt to file the motion. Because Mr. Mersel made a conscious decision to wait until the final hour to file his motion, he assumed the risk that on October 10, his luck would run out…

> Judge Cormac J. Carney, USDC,
> Southern District of California

———————————

The consequences of an untimely filing can be severe. As Judge Easeterbrook once wrote,

Courts used to say that a single day's delay can cost a litigant valuable rights. With e-filing, one hour's or even a minute's delay can cost a litigant valuable rights. A prudent litigant or lawyer must allow time for difficulties on the filer's end. A crash of the lawyer's computer, or a power outage at 11:50 PM, does not extend the deadline, even though unavailability of the court's computer can do so under Rule 6(a)(3).[61]

Given the crucial importance of filing deadlines, it's no wonder some attorneys go to elaborate and almost comical lengths to avoid a late filing. Take, for example, a handful of attorneys from Snell & Wilmer, whose trademarked motto was "Character Comes Through."[62] These attorneys engaged in the perverse practice of pre-stamping filings using a courthouse time-stamp and then filing the pre-stamped briefs late. When caught, they received this gentle but humiliating benchslap from Judge Dale Kimball of Utah's Central Division:

> It has come to the court's attention at least twice during the past few months that the "date filed" stamp on certain of Yamaha's pleadings does not correspond with the date on which that pleading is actually placed in the court's outside drop box. When first notified about this problem, the court declined to take any action, hoping that such an event was an isolated incident. But it has happened again.
>
> Specifically, it appears that Yamaha's counsel or counsel's agent has been, on occasion, date-stamping the first page of the document to be filed (or the envelope in which the documents is placed), using the court's time stamp located outside the building near the after-hours drop box. The document, however, is not actually placed in the drop box at that time.
>
> For example, at 10:11 p.m. on Friday, February 16, 2007, Yamaha purportedly "filed" "Defendant Yamaha Motor Corporation USA's Reply Memorandum in Support of Objection to Order Denying Motion for Leave to Reopen Disocvery [sic] Regarding Newly Disclosed Evidence" and

"Declaration of Angela Stander in Support of Defendant Yamaha Motor Corporation USA's Reply Memorandum in Support of Objection to Order Denying Motion for Leave to Reopen Disocvery [sic] Regarding Newly Disclosed Evidence." Because of the President's Day holiday, the drop box was not emptied by court staff until the morning of Tuesday, February 20, 2007. Yamaha's documents, however, were not located in the drop box at that time. Rather, the documents were located in the drop box when it was emptied on the following morning – Wednesday, February 21, 2007. Indeed, the documents were sandwiched between documents from other cases that were filed during the night of February 20, 2007. It is clear that the documents were not "filed" with the court until four days after the "filed" stamp was applied to the documents. This is at least the second time that such conduct has been discovered by court staff.

This deceitful conduct will not be tolerated. The conduct is particularly egregious when counsel has been previously notified that the court is liberal in granting extensions of time when additional time is needed. Moreover, counsel in this case have been admonished before about the gamesmanship that has been taking place in this lawsuit . . .

> "This deceitful conduct will not be tolerated."

Accordingly, counsel is hereby notified that, if any such conduct is again observed by court staff, the court will strike the documents(s) at issue and therefore will not consider the document(s) in deciding any related motion. Additionally, counsel for both parties are hereby notified that they are not to electronically file any "Notice of Conventional Filing" until after the document actually has been filed with the court. Regarding the two specific documents mentioned above, the Clerk of the Court is directed to enter the filing date as "February 20, 2007," notwithstanding the "filed" stamp of February 16, 2007.

Judge Dale Kimball, Central Division, Utah

———————————

Judge Kimball's published opinion was restrained, but the conduct it described was embarrassing both to the attorneys involved and to the law firm of Snell & Wilmer, a prestigious practice with nine offices across the western United States. The firm responded to Judge Kimball's rebuke with this obsequious letter from lead counsel Tracy Howler, followed by an internal investigation and a personal court appearance by the firm's managing partner, Alan Sullivan.

The Honorable Dale A. Kimball
United States District Court Judge
350 South Main Street, Room 222
Salt Lake City, Utah 84101

　　　　Re:　　*Boss Industries v. Yamaha Motor Corporation USA;* Case No. CV-05-422 DAK

Dear Judge Kimball:

　　　　This letter is a preliminary response to the Order entered on Wednesday, February 28, 2007 in the Boss case. I was shocked and embarrassed by the events described in the Order. I had no personal involvement in the filing or service of the documents in question but, of course, I am responsible as lead counsel for the actions taken by those working under my supervision.

　　　　Upon review of the Order, I advised Alan Sullivan, the managing partner in our office, and other senior partners here about the situation. Mr. Sullivan is undertaking a thorough investigation and we will report the firm's conclusions to the Court as soon as possible.

　　　　I want to underscore for the Court that I have never engaged in the type of conduct described in the Court's Order and would never condone or tolerate such conduct by anyone working with me. My partners share with me the strong feeling that such conduct would be completely unacceptable. You have my word that no such event will ever occur in this case or any other in which I am involved. I apologize to you and to the Court's staff for the inconvenience and frustration that arises from a situation like this.

　　　　　　　　　　　　Sincerely,

　　　　　　　　　　　　SNELL & WILMER L.L.P.

　　　　　　　　　　　　Tracy H. Fowler

THF:gjb
cc:　　Alan Anderson, Esq., via U.S. mail
　　　　Margaret McGann, Esq., via U.S. mail
　　　　William Shreve, Esq., via U.S. mail

The behavior in the above case seems so extreme, and so bizarre, that one would think it's unique. One would be wrong. In fact, the hapless attorneys from Snell & Wilmer were not even the first to try this particular ruse. The pressure on attorneys to produce good work product within a short timeframe can drive even the brightest and most talented minds in the industry into the realm of temporary insanity, during which they will do whatever they must for just a few extra days' time to file.

Case in point is Alison "Sunny" Maynard, a hard-working public interest attorney from Colorado. (Her adversaries might hasten to argue she's also an unrepentant legal conspiracy theorist, but the substance of Ms. Maynard's legal arguments is beyond the scope of this book.) Ms. Maynard is no slouch. She graduated from Cornell University with a degree in physics and then worked two years as a geophysicist for an oil company before attending law school. After graduating from law school she served in Colorado as Deputy District Attorney, Assistant Attorney General and City Attorney before entering private practice. In 2002, she even ran for Colorado Attorney General on the Green Party ticket. A number of Ms. Maynard's clients seek her representation in public interest litigation and she assists them on a *pro bono* or reduced fee basis.

Based on her resume, Ms. Maynard isn't someone readers would expect to engage in peculiar and unethical behavior. And yet, as described below in a Colorado Supreme Court order imposing sanctions, she did exactly that; and all to gain just four days of extra time to file an opening brief:

Respondent [Allison Maynard's] opening brief was originally due on May 8, 2007. However, on March 8, 2007, Respondent filed a "Motion for One-Week Extension." The Supreme Court granted her request and set a new due date of May 15, 2007. Thereafter, Respondent made four additional requests to extend the filing date of her brief and the Supreme Court granted each request. However, on March 25, 2007, the Supreme Court entered an order with the following written admonition, "NO FURTHER EXTENSIONS." With this final extension, the Supreme Court gave Respondent until June 19, 2007 to complete her brief.

Although the Supreme Court admonished her that no further extensions would be granted, Respondent failed to complete the brief by June 19, 2007. From March 25, 2007 until June 19, 2007, a period of 86 days, Respondent worked on CPA's brief and other client matters, but admittedly gave no particular priority to CPA's brief.

With the final deadline looming, Respondent realized that she would be unable to complete her brief on time. While she had worked approximately forty hours on the brief and had completed a draft at that point, she was dissatisfied with its quality. Aside from the task of completing the written brief, Respondent testified that she had to contend with a disorganized and voluminous record from the water court in the CPA appeal. Despite her concerns about completing the brief by June 19, 2007, Respondent failed to advise the Supreme Court of her inability to complete the brief in a timely manner.

Instead of filing the draft she completed at that point, she contemplated a means by which she could submit it after the Court's deadline.

Following the final deadline, June 19, 2007, Respondent worked approximately 36 additional hours on the brief and filed it with the Supreme Court on June 23, 2007. However, in order to make the brief appear to be timely filed, Respondent placed a stamp she purchased on June 19, 2007 on the envelope containing her brief and mailed it to the Supreme Court. The stamp, which she purchased from an automated machine, bore the date of June 19, 2007. She kept the receipt and later supplied it to the Supreme Court as proof that she had in fact mailed and filed her brief on June 19, 2007 as the Court ordered.

In addition, Respondent certified on the final page of her brief that she had mailed it on June 19, 2007. In these proceedings, Respondent testified that she rationalized her duplicity by "compartmentalizing" in her mind her deceitfulness and focused solely on the goal of providing a quality brief on behalf of CPA.

> "Respondent testified that she rationalized her duplicity by 'compartmentalizing' in her mind her deceitfulness and focused solely on the goal of providing a quality brief..."

Nevertheless, Respondent knew her conduct in deceiving the Court was unethical.

On June 22, 2007, the United States of America and other parties to the appeal ("appellees") filed a motion to dismiss CPA's appeal for failure to file an opening brief and for failure to prosecute the appeal.

In their motion, the appellees stated that as of June 22, 2007, Respondent had not filed her brief. They therefore requested that her appeal be dismissed for failure to prosecute.

On or about June 25, 2007, the Supreme Court clerk received and date-stamped Respondent's "Response to Motion to Dismiss Appeal." In response to her opponent's motion to dismiss the appeal, Respondent made the following written misrepresentations and false statements to the Supreme Court in an effort to demonstrate that she had indeed filed her brief on June 19, 2000:

"I mailed the opening brief to the Court and obtained a postmark on the due date, June 19, 2007. Rule 25(a)(1), C.A.R., says, '[B]riefs shall be deemed filed on the day of mailing if the most expeditious form of delivery by mail, excepting delivery, is utilized.' The briefs were sent by Priority Mail. See the receipt attached as Exhibit A."

"I admit I did not effect service on the parties until the evening of June 20, so am herewith filing an amended certificate of service. I consent in advance to the Appellee's taking three extra days in its response, due to the delay."

"WHEREFORE, the brief having been timely filed, according to the rules, Appellee's motion to dismiss appeal must be denied."

On June 25, 2007, the Supreme Court received and stamped Respondent's Amended Certificate of Service. In her amended certificate of service, Respondent asserted that she had mailed her brief to the parties on June 20, and not on June 19 as she had originally alleged. In fact, Respondent did not obtain service of the opening brief on the parties on June 19 or 20, 2007, and her statement to that effect was knowingly and intentionally false.

Respondent eventually contacted Philip Doe, the president of CPA, and notified him that she had filed CPA's appellate brief with the Supreme Court by misrepresenting to them that her brief was timely filed when it was not. Respondent thereafter decided to advise the Supreme Court of her subterfuge. Respondent first called the Supreme Court to find out if her brief had been accepted. Respondent testified that when the clerk of the Supreme Court told her the brief had been accepted; Respondent admitted to the clerk she had not timely filed the brief.

On June 28, 2007, immediately following her conversation with the clerk, Respondent filed an "Admission; and Motion for Last Extension, or Withdrawal of Brief" with the Supreme Court. In her motion, Respondent stated as follows:

The undersigned attorney for Appellant Citizens' Progressive Alliance ("CPA") hereby informs the court that I did not mail the opening brief on June 19, 2007, as represented, because it was not finished. Instead, I purchased a postage meter stamp at the automated postage center on that day; and, when I finished the brief on Saturday, June 23, used that postage to mail it at that time. In the same fashion, I purchased postage for service on the parties on June 20, and filed an amended certificate of service to that effect; their briefs were not mailed until Saturday, June 23, either.

The reason for the misrepresentation was that I was "boxed in" obviously, with an order saying no further extensions; had a duty to my client to get the brief in; and was simply not done, the main reason being the record of these two old cases, 1751-B and 807-C, which is a nightmare. I wanted to get to the bottom of what happened with these cases, which led to entry of the original decree for ALP. So, I made a misrepresentation to the Court. I have realized, of course, that that makes me no better than a lot of people I have complained about in my time, including particularly Judge Eakes in the ALP cases, who, as the Court will learn when it reads the brief (if it does), altered a number of court documents.

I have always taken the moral high road, and clients come to me, and reported that they have done so, because (as one told me recently) I have a reputation of incorruptibility. I want to keep it that way, so am making a clean breast of it to the Court about what I did. Before filing this this morning, I also told my client Phil Doe what I had done and, while realizing the consequences which could result, he

> "My client told me, 'Experience keeps a dear school but a fool learn no other.'"

said, "People in the heat of battle often do things they regret." He also told me, however, that "Experience keeps a dear school but a fool learn no other."

I request a last extension from the Court, out of time, on the brief, through Saturday, June 23, warranted because of the state of the court record. I also commit to obtain counseling so that I can overcome this problem I have of not getting my work done on time. Should the Court not forgive this offense, and grant the extension, I withdraw the brief.]

By order dated July 2, 2007, the Supreme Court granted appellee's motion to dismiss CPA's appeal.

————————————

Ms. Maynard was ultimately disbarred for her sad but funny behavior, which gained her only four days of extra time to finish her brief on top of the previous extensions already granted by the Colorado Supreme Court. Her deception and failure to file a timely opening brief also caused her appeal to be dismissed, preventing her client from challenging adverse decisions from lower courts. Despite acknowledging her misconduct to the Supreme Court, Ms. Maynard appears to believe her elaborate ruse to mislead the court was not sufficient grounds for dismissal and was mere procedural "pretext" by the Court. (In fairness to the Colorado Supreme Court, it's hard to imagine any court in the country would permit a litigant to proceed under the circumstances described above.) In May 2010, Ms. Maynard[ii] made the following blog post on a website advocating removal of Colorado's Supreme Court Justices:

> Case 06 SA 388 [,the case discussed in the excerpt above,] was the appeal dismissed on a pretext: *I was denied a last four-day extension on my opening brief in this case, despite the fact that the project had been sitting around for 50 years, and my appeal was dismissed.* This was the Animas-La Plata diligence case (water rights). I revealed numerous instances of fraud in my brief... [63] (emphasis added)

Ms. Maynard's comment neglects to mention *why* the Colorado Supreme Court refused to grant her extension and instead, in lengthy fashion, makes clear her opinion the case was dismissed solely on account of political jockeying and a corrupt judiciary. Perhaps unsurprisingly, the rules violation described above was not Ms. Maynard's first. She is well-known to frequenters of legal blogs for a classic motion filed and later withdrawn in the same matter while it was still in a lower court.

> Opposer Citizens Progressive Alliance ("CPA"), through its attorney undersigned and pursuant to Rule 6(b)(2), C.R.C.P., respectfully requests another one-day extension, to Monday,

---

ii Or at least someone representing him- or herself to be Ms. Maynard.

March 5, 2007, to respond to the Applicant's (and other opposers') bills of costs. As grounds therefor, the undersigned states that she had almost completed this response on the due date, which was Friday, March 2, but suspended her work in order to take a friend out to dinner for his birthday. When she came back, she was unable to finish it, due to the wine. :-) The response is filed herewith.

WHEREFORE, inebriation constituting excusable neglect, and no prejudice inuring to the other parties, the court should grant the present extension, as it is in the interest of justice.[64]

For those who rightly question the veracity of the pleading, this author confirmed the actual document filed in Utah state court by an experienced and accomplished attorney did, in fact, contain a smiley-face emoticon. The document was posted on legal blog Above the Law and Ms. Maynard subsequently "bombarded" the editors with unpleasant e-mails. As noted by David Lat, Above the Law's Editor-in Chief: "How can we reconcile this deadly earnest, possibly paranoid environmental crusader with the fun-loving, wine-swilling, emoticon-using lawyer who filed such a delightful and charming motion?"[65] How, indeed? This is the type of question that keeps this author up nights.

While Ms. Maynard clearly struggles to meet deadlines, others in the legal profession struggle to stay within page limits. Justice LeRoy Millette of the Virginia Supreme Court once noted that when he receives a brief, the first thing he does is flip to the last page to check the length.[66] One of his colleagues is rumored to have chastened a litigant by stating that "page limits are not guidelines."[67] These Justices are not alone in their obsession with the length of pleadings.

In 1979, at the dawn of the modern benchslap, retired Chief Judge John R. Brown of the Fifth Circuit drafted a blistering smack down for counsels' oversized filings in *Gordon v. Green*, which included the classic sub-headings, "The Pleadings: Gobbledeygook," and "'Let They Speech Be Short, Comprehending Much in Few Words.'"[68] The opinion is entertaining, but the footnotes are gems:

> The various complaints, amendments, amended amendments, amendments to amended amendments, and other related papers are anything but short, totaling over 4,000 pages, occupying 18 volumes, and requiring a hand truck or cart to move. [Footnote 6: Appellant's filings demonstrate once and for all that history does in fact repeat itself. In discussing Dr. J. H. Baker's second volume of Spelman's Reports, the 1978 Report of the Council and Abstract of the Accounts of the Selden Society reveals (p. 6): "It is in the Sixth century that the sheer physical bulk of the [plea] rolls [became] truly daunting, with a mile or two of parchment used in a term." If every party filed the massive pleadings submitted here, we would only hasten the speed at which our country's trees are being transformed into sheets of legal jargon. Moreover, we would need to build another courthouse simply to store legal documents.] The Court also observed that a paragraph from one typical complaint was single spaced, "extend[ed] the full length of a legal page and constitute[d] a single sentence." Much of the pleadings are scandalous as well. [Footnote 7: At the risk of further polluting the legal waters by immortalizing this gibberish in the annals of the Federal

Reporter, we quote some of the typically scandalous language from one of appellant's many filings:

> "At the risk of further polluting the legal waters by immortalizing this gibberish in the annals of the Federal Reporter, we quote some of the typically scandalous language."

Green and Broberg worked closely together to keep their grandiose "Money making monster" scheme in operation ... (3) by forcing the investors in various syndications to continue to make payments through the loyalty and enthusiasm of those investors who had compromised themselves to the scheme by making money by means of the Green-Broberg scheme, ... Broberg aided and abetted Green in actively working to police compliance with the "pay or you are out of the deal completely" enforcement concept in this scheme that can only be described as diabolical and monstrous, by Broberg's legal advice that he forfeiture clause was legal (thus Broberg bears an awesome burden towards the investors because of his special fiduciary responsibilities as an Attorney at Law), (4) by not only failing to register this securities investment scheme to bring it under the supervision and censure of the S.E.C. but to openly operate in what was, in fact, an outlaw fashion, based on the spurious so-called "legal opinion" of Attorney Broberg, rendered to investors and potential investors, to the effect that this scheme did *not* constitute securities but that, on the contrary, it was simple country-style real estate with lots of country-style profit in it for all collaborators, but destructions for the defector who will be cannibalized by the rest of the group, again based on the so-called "legal opinion" of Broberg to the effect that failure to make payments for whatever reasons constitutes a breach of the so-called "trust agreement" and subjects the defector to losing his entire interest and having it assumed (cannibalized) by the remaining investors . . .

Moreover, we cannot tell whether complaints filed earlier in time are to be read in conjunction with those filed later or whether the amended versions supersede previous pleadings. . .

One option is to struggle through the thousands of pages of pleadings in an effort to determine (assuming we possibly could) whether the Trial Court correctly dismissed for lack of jurisdiction. However, such a course of action would be unwise from the standpoint of sound judicial administration. All would know that there is no longer any necessity for paying the least bit heed to F.R.Civ.P. 8(a) in its demand for "a short and plain statement" reiterated by the 8(e) requirement that each averment "be simple, concise, and direct." Lawyers would see that in the face of even gross violations of Rule 8, we would undertake the burden of trying to parse out 18 volumes of words, disorganized and sometimes conflicting, with a mish-mash of so-called evidentiary materials, citations or authority, and other things that a pleader, aware of an faithful to the command of Federal Rules of Civil Procedure, knows to be completely extraneous. And the District Courts who come on the firing line are the first victims of the paper mill. We think that the Trial Court should have dismissed the complaints with leave to amend. While a Trial Court is and should be given great leeway in determining whether a party has complied with Rule 8, we think that as a matter of law, verbose and scandalous pleadings of over 4,000 pages violate Rule 8. . .

We fully agree with the observation of the District Court for the Eastern District of Michigan that "the law does not require, nor does justice demand, that a judge must grope through [thousands of] pages of irrational, prolix and redundant pleadings." *Passic v. State*, 98 F.Supp. 1015, 1016 (E.D. Mich, 1951.

Our view – that flagrant violations of Rule 8 should not be tolerated – is shared by Courts throughout the country. . . If our holding results in more time and expense to appellant, that would be fair recompense for these marked, unjustifiable violations of the letter and spirit of the Federal Rules of Civil Procedure and an indifference as though they had never been adopted 41 years ago. [Footnote 13: Counsel as scrivener would have been fair game for the discipline meted out by the Chancellor in 1596. As Professor Richard C. Wydick of Davis Law School reports: "In 1596 an English chancellor decided to make an example of a particularly prolix document filed in his court. The chancellor first ordered a hole cut through the center of the document, all 120 pages of it. Then he ordered that the person who wrote it should have his head stuffed through the hole, and the unfortunate fellow was led around to be exhibited to all those attending court at West Minister Hall." Obviously this applies only to counsel who filed the papers, not to the appellate counsel who briefed and argued the case here.

> "The chancellor ordered a hole cut through the center of the document … and ordered that the person who wrote it should have his head stuffed through the hole… to be exhibited to all those attending court at West Minister Hall."

Chief Judge John R. Brown, Fifth Circuit

While 16th century benchslaps were clearly more painful than modern benchslaps, Chief Judge Brown's opinion was equally humiliating. And his opinion is just one of many that bemoan unnecessarily lengthy pleadings.[iii] In her excellent article entitled *Bareheaded and Barefaced Counsel: Courts React to Unprofessionalism in Lawyers' Papers*,[69] Professor Judith D. Fischer

---

[iii] *See, e.g., Frazier v. Columbus Bd. of Educ.*, 70 Ohio St. 3d 1431, 1431, 638 N.E.2d 581, 581 (1994) (striking excessively long memorandum and dismissing case); *Staffilino Chevrolet, Inc. v. Ohio Motor Vehicle Dealers Bd.*, 60 Ohio St. 3d 1486, 1486, 635 N.E.2d 41, 41 (1994) (dismissing case because of length of memorandum); *N/S Corp. v. Liberty Mut. Ins, Co.*, No. 96-55641, 1997 WL 656358, at *1 (Ninth Cir. Oct. 23, 1997) (dismissing case for breach of multiple rules, including word limit); *Columbus-America Discovery Group v. Atlantic Mut. Ins. Co.*, 56 F.3d 556, 574 n.23 (Fourth Cir. 1995) (refusing to consider pages exceeding limit); *Conkling v. Turner*, 18 F.3d 1285, 1299 (Fifth Cir. 1994) (disallowing arguments saved for reply brief in attempt to evade page limit); *State v. Hudson*, 123 N.C. Ct. App. 336, 338, 473 S.E.2d 415, 417 (1996) (fining lawyer $500 for submitting 42-page brief where limit was 35 pages), rev'd on other grounds; *State v. Armijo*, 118 N.M. 802, 814, 887 P.2d 1269, 1281 n.2 (1994) (mentioning possible future sanctions for excessive pages in briefs); Alex Kozinski, *The Wrong Stuff*, 1992 B.Y.U. L. Rev. 325, 326 (1992) (implying long briefs lack strong arguments and are harmful to cases); *Kano v. National Consumer Co-op. Bank*, 22 F.3d 899, 899-00 (Ninth Cir. 1994) (levying $1,500 in sanctions for circumventing page limit); *Westinghouse Electric Corp. v. NLRB*, 809 F.2d 419, 424-25 (Seventh Cir. 1987) (forbidding lawyers from passing on to clients $1,000 in sanctions based on page limit evasion); *Doyle v. Hasbro, Inc.*, 103 F.3d. 186, 196 (First Cir. 1996) (assessing double costs for attempt to "flaunt the page limits" through improper line spacing); *United Automobile, Aerospace & Agricultural Implement Workers v. NLRB*, Nos. 88-7297, 88-7374 & 88-7510, 1990 WL 61309, at *4 (Ninth Cir. May 11, 1990) (imposing $500 sanctions for circumventing page limits by improper spacing); *In re MacIntyre*, 181 B.R. 420, 421-22 (Ninth Cir. 1995) (sanctioning counsel $250 for using "minuscule" type to circumvent page limits); *State v. Walden*, 183 Ariz. 595, 605, 905 P.2d 974, 984 (1995) (finding waiver of issues included in amended brief's appendix in order to circumvent page limit).

notes an opinion by the New York Court of Appeals that dedicated several pages to "comment on a matter that concerns us greatly, namely, the quality, length and content of briefs presented to this court."[70] The court observed that it often receives "poorly written and excessively long briefs, replete with burdensome, irrelevant, and immaterial matter," and that counsel in the current case "wander(ed) aimlessly through myriad irrelevant matters of administrative and constitutional law, pausing only briefly to discuss the issues raised by this appeal." Aggravating his violation, counsel included at the end of his 284-page pleading a four-page explanation of why the brief was so long.

The Third Circuit Court of Appeals has dismissed appeals for violating briefing rules, particularly because those rules are "carefully drafted to assist a court burdened with a heavy case load."[71] The Ninth Circuit once dismissed an appeal when appellant "approached our rules with such insouciance that we cannot overlook its needlessness."[72]

When an attorney filed an oversized brief without receiving prior approval from the court, District Court Judge Steven Merryday issued the following benchslap, which included a redlined version of plaintiff's original pleading.

On August 3, 2012, the plaintiffs moved (Doc. 22) for leave to submit a motion that exceeds the page limit. The motion states, "The complex factual and legal issues involved[] make it difficult to meet the page limitation of twenty-five [] pages." Two hours later and without leave, the plaintiffs submitted (Doc. 23) a twenty-nine-page motion. Based on the mistaken premise that this FLSA collective action presents atypically complex issues, the motion to exceed the page limit (Doc. 22) is DENIED. The motion for conditional collective status (Doc. 23) is STRICKEN.

A review of the proposed, twenty-nine-page motion's commencement confirms that a modicum of informed editorial revision easily reduces the motion to twenty-five pages without a reduction in substance. Compare this:

> Plaintiffs~~, ZACHARY BELLI, BENJAMIN PETERSON, ERIC KINSLEY, and LARRY JOHNSON, (hereinafter referred to as "Plaintiffs"), individually and on behalf of all others similarly situated ("Class members"), by and through the undersigned counsel and pursuant to the Fair Labor Standards Act of 1938, (the "FLSA"), 29 U.S.C. § 216(b) files this motion seeking an order~~ [move] (1) [to] conditionally certif~~ying this case as~~ a collective ~~class~~ action; (2) [to] requir[e]~~ing~~ the Defendant~~, HEDDEN ENTERPRISES, INC. d/b/a INFINITY TECHNOLOGY SOLUTIONS (hereinafter "Defendant")~~, to produce ~~and disclose all of~~ the names[,] ~~and last known~~ addresses[,] and telephone numbers of the [each] potential ~~C~~[c]lass ~~M~~[m]embers ~~so that notice may be implemented~~; and (3) [to] authoriz[e]~~ing~~ notice ~~by U.S. First Class mail to all~~ [of this action to each] similarly situated persons employed by Defendant within ~~the past~~ three ~~(3)~~ years[.] ~~to inform them of the pendency of this suit and to inform them of their right to opt-in to this lawsuit. In support of this Motion, Plaintiffs sets forth the following facts and provides this Court with a Memorandum of Law in support of the Motion, and asserts as follows:~~

To this:

> Plaintiffs move (1) to conditionally certify a collective action; (2) to require the Defendant to produce the name, address, and telephone number of each potential class member; and (3) to authorize notice of this action to each similarly situated person employed by Defendant within three years.

Concentrating on the elimination of redundancy, verbosity, and legalism (*see, e.g.,* BRYAN A. GARNER, THE ELEMENTS OF LEGAL STYLE (2d ed. 2002)), the plaintiffs may submit a twenty-five-page motion on or before August 15, 2012.[73]

Judge Steven D. Merrday, USDC
Middle District of Florida

————————————

Rambling pleadings have been earning stern benchslaps from courts for more than 400 years, and with good reason. But violating page limits is often a symptom of other, more pressing performance issues: laziness, ignorance or incompetence. These more fundamental problems come to the fore in the following chapters.

CHAPTER 6: Writing Rage

Exceeding a page limit and other formatting violations are technical errors that often reflect a more substantive problem: poor writing. Judges are willing to accept over-sized briefs when necessary to make a persuasive argument. But more often than not, lengthy briefs are unnecessary and simply require extra work for the judge.

Judges are sensitive to attorneys' work-product because writing is at the heart of the legal profession. They care deeply about organization, prose, grammar, syntax, phrasing, tone and style. Each year they read thousands of pleadings regarding diverse issues, with complicated facts and dense legal arguments. A sure way to engender a judge's affection is to use clear and concise language in a well-organized brief; a sure way to enrage a judge to is to use clumsy, rambling or imprecise prose. Even the misuse of a single word can affect a judge's opinion.

Consider Judge Ronald L. Bauer's response to counsel's misuse of the word "piecemeal" in a memorandum:

The court's search of the etymology of the word 'piecemeal' has revealed that there are two characters in Marvel Comics that bear the name Piecemeal, including one who is an adversary of the Incredible Hulk. The word can also be used as an adjective or an adverb. But nowhere has the court found that this word is properly used as a verb. Yet counsel here have argued at length about whether or not the District improperly 'piecemealed' the closure and reuse of O'Neill. Perhaps this word will one day achieve that status, and counsel can take pride at being midwives for that birth, but the court will, for now, adhere to more traditional terms.[74]

Judge Ronald L. Bauer, Orange County Superior Court

–––––––––––––––––––––

Little things matter, especially in the law. Nothing could appear less significant than minor grammar, spelling and punctuation errors. But cases, contracts and millions of dollars have hinged on single commas, misplaced pronouns and inconsistent clauses.

Grammar and Keyboarding _____

Poor grammar is a continual source of judicial benchslaps. Sometimes, benchslaps for poor grammar are minor. In *Sanches v. Carrolton-Farmers Branch Independent School Dist.*, the court simply noted in a footnote that:

Usually we do not comment on technical and grammatical errors, because anyone can make such an occasional mistake,

123

but here the miscues are so egregious and obvious that an average fourth grader would have avoided most of them. For example, the word "principals" should have been "principles." The word "vacatur" is misspelled. The subject and verb are not in agreement in one of the sentences, which has a singular subject ("incompetence") and a plural verb ("are"). Magistrate Judge Stickney is referred to as "it" instead of "he" and is called a "magistrate" instead of a "magistrate judge." And finally, the sentence containing the word "incompetence" makes no sense as a matter of standard English prose, so it is not reasonably possible to understand the thought, if any, that is being conveyed. It is ironic that the term "incompetence" is used here, because the only thing that is incompetent is the passage itself.[75]

Judge Jerry E. Smith, Fifth Circuit

———————————

Other times, smack downs for poor grammar can be staggering. Justice J.J. Robertson of Mississippi's Supreme Court once lambasted a local district attorney for an indictment that was "grammatically unintelligible" such that "not even Shakespeare" could have understood it. Justice Robertson's opinion highlights a case of legalese at its worst:

> "This case presents the question of whether the rules of English grammar are a part of the positive law of the state."

This case presents the question of whether the rules of English grammar are a part of the positive law of this state. If they are, Jacob Henderson's burglary conviction must surely be reversed, for the indictment in which he has been charged would receive an "F" from every English teacher in the land.

Though grammatically unintelligible, we find that the indictment is legally sufficient and affirm, knowing full well that our decision will receive of literate persons everywhere opprobrium as intense and widespread as it will be deserved...

The primary issue presented on this appeal regards the legal adequacy of the indictment under which Henderson has been tried, convicted and sentenced. That indictment, in pertinent part, reads as follows:

The Grand Jurors for the State of Mississippi, ... upon their oaths present: That Jacob Henderson ... on the 1Fifth day of May, A.D., 1982.

The store building there situated, the property of Metro Auto Painting, Inc., ... in which store building was kept for sale or use valuable things, to-wit: goods, ware and merchandise unlawfully, feloniously and burglariously did break and enter, with intent the goods, wares and merchandise of said Metro Auto Painting then and there being in said store building unlawfully, feloniously and then and there being in said store building burglariously to take, steal and carry away; And

One (1) Polaroid Land Camera,

One (1) Realistic AM/FM Stereo Tuner

One (1) Westminster AM/FM radio

One (1) Metal Box and contents thereof, ...

the property of the said Metro Auto Painting then and there being in said store building did then and there unlawfully, feloniously and burglariously take, steal and carry away the aforesaid property, he, the said Jacob Henderson, having been twice previously convicted of felonies, to-wit: ...

The remainder of the indictment charges Henderson with being a recidivist.

Henderson, no doubt offended, demurred. In support, he presented an expert witness, Ann Dreher, who had been a teacher of English for nine years. Ms. Dreher testified that, when read consistent with accepted rules of English grammar, the indictment did not charge Jacob Henderson with doing anything; rather it charged that goods, ware and merchandise broke and entered the paint store. The trial judge overruled the objection and the motion, but not without reservation. He stated:

> [T]his same objection has been made numerous times. It is one of Mr. Hailey's pets. [B]ut as far as I know no one has elected to appeal and I'm going to follow the decision whether it is grammatically correct or not. I have repeatedly begged for six years or five years for the district attorney not to use this form. It is very poor English. It is impossible English... In addition to being very poor English, it also charges him with the crime of

larceny, which is not necessary to include in an indictment for burglary. I never did understand the reason for that. I again ask the district attorney not to use this form. It's archaic. Even Shakespeare could not understand the grammatical construction of this indictment. But the objection will be overruled. Maybe it will take a reversal on a case of a similar nature where there is a serious offense as this one is by the fact that he is indicted as a habitual to get the district attorney's attention.

> "Even Shakespeare could not understand the grammatical construction of this indictment."

In the trial court and on this appeal, Henderson insists that the meaning of the indictment may be obtained only within the strait jacket of accepted rules of grammatical construction of the English language. From this point of view, we are asked to examine the indictment and concentrate on the words "... unlawfully, feloniously and burglariously did break and enter ...." Who, we are asked, when the rules of good grammar are employed, did this alleged breaking and entering?

There are two possible answers (again, looking at the indictment as would an English teacher). "Goods, ware and merchandise" are the most obvious choice. Those nouns proximately precede the verb(s) "did break and enter" (separated only by the familiar string of adverbs "unlawfully, feloniously and burglariously"-the district attorney, like other lawyers, never uses one word when two or three will do just as well). Thus read, the indictment charges that Goods, ware and merchandise, not Jacob Henderson, burglarized the Maaco Paint Shop on May 15, 1982.

More properly, however, the words "Goods, ware and merchandise" are seen as the tail end of a largely unintelligible effort to describe something else: the store building. A perceptive English grammarian would conclude that it is "the store building there situated..." which is charged with the burglary, for those words seem to constitute the subject of the nonsensical non-sentence we are charged to construe.

Even so, whether the indictment charges that "Goods, ware and merchandise" *or* "The store building there situated" ... "unlawfully, feloniously and burglariously did break and enter ..." matters not to Jacob Henderson. His point is merely that the indictment does *not* charge that *he* did the breaking and entering.

Were this a Court of nine English teachers, Henderson no doubt would prevail.

The indictment does contain at the outset the charge "That Jacob Henderson ... on the 1Fifth day of May, A.D., 1982." We have another non-sentence. The unmistakable period after 1982 is used by astute defense counsel to nail down the point - that the indictment fails to charge that Jacob Henderson did anything on May 15, 1982. Again, we must concede that grammatically speaking counsel is correct. The period after 1982 grammatically precludes the possibility that the indictment charges that Jacob Henderson did break and enter. Either the words "did break and enter" would have to precede the period, or the name Jacob Henderson would have to appear following it. Neither is the case.

Recognizing that the period is important, the State argues that in reality the indictment consists of one long sentence, written albeit in legalese instead of English. The State argues that "the period grammatically disjoined the first part of the sentence from the second", conceding that we are indeed confronted with "a patently inappropriate period". This, of course, prompts Henderson to analogize the state's argument to Lady Macbeth's famous "Out damned spot! Out, I say!" [Footnote 1: It cannot be gainsaid that all the perfumes of Arabia would not eviscerate the grammatical stench emanating from this indictment. Cf. W. Shakespeare, Macbeth, Act V, sc. 1, lines 56-57.] W. Shakespeare, Macbeth, Act V, sc. 1, line 38. The retort would be telling in the classroom or in a court of the literati. Alas, it has meager force in a court of law…

Establishment of a literate bar is a worthy aspiration. 'Tis without doubt a consummation devoutly to be wished. Its achievement, however, must be relegated to means other than reversal of criminal convictions justly and lawfully secured.

> "Establishment of a literate bar is a worthy aspiration."

The assignment of error is rejected…[76]

Justice J.J. Robertson, Supreme Court of Mississippi

———————————————

Although most judges and attorneys are united in their opposition to legalese, it is a difficult practice to upset. One reason is that many new lawyers, short on experience and devoid of legal writing skills, rely on a hodgepodge of boilerplate forms rather than learning how to draft original pleadings. Templates and forms are inherited from prior generations of attorneys and each subsequent generation mutilates what might have been, once upon a time, a perfectly good legal document. Blind and repeated reliance on forms usually results in pleadings that are unintelligible. Case in point is David W. Glasser, an attorney from Daytona, Florida who received this humiliating benchslap from District Court Judge Gregory Presnell:

> This matter came before the Court without oral argument upon consideration of Plaintiff's, Carolyn Nault ("Plaintiff"), Response to this Court's Order and Motion for Voluntary Dismissal (collectively, the "Motion") (Docs. 21 and 22). Upon review, it is ORDERED that the Motion is DENIED without prejudice for failing to comply with Local Rule 3.01(g), for failing to secure a stipulation of dismissal from Defendant pursuant to FED.R. CIV. 41(a)(ii), and for otherwise being riddled with unprofessional grammatical and typographical errors that nearly render the entire Motion incomprehensible.

"It is further ordered that Plaintiff's counsel ... shall re-read the Local Rules and the Federal Rules of Civil Procedure in their entirety."

It is FURTHER ORDERED that Plaintiff's counsel, David W. Glasser, shall re-read the Local Rules and the Federal Rules of Civil Procedure in their entirety. Furthermore, Mr. Glasser shall personally hand deliver a copy of this Order, together with the

Court's exhibit attached thereto, to his client, Carolyn Nault, by no later than Monday, September 21, 2009. By no later than Wednesday, September 23, 2009, Mr. Glasser shall file with the Court a "Notice of Compliance," certifying to the Court that he has fully complied with this Order.[77]

Judge Gregory Presnell, USDC,
Middle District of Florida

––––––––––––––––––––––––

Adding insult to injury, the "exhibit attached thereto" was Judge Presnell's hand-corrected copy of Mr. Glasser's pleadings. In fairness to Mr. Glasser, he had been successfully practicing law for over 23 years before receiving Judge Presnell's much-publicized benchslap (he is a 1988 graduate of the "Nova Southeastern University Shepard Broad Law Center," an accredited law school with nearly 1,000 enrolled students).[78] While Mr. Glasser's pleadings were riddled with grammatical and typographical errors, the documents were at least substantively intelligible. This author has encountered worse during his brief practice. But Mr. Glasser's smack down illustrates how even experienced attorneys making routine filings are at risk of a benchslap if they encounter a judge on a bad day.

Spelling and Punctuation _____

Mr. Glasser's crime was poor grammar and keyboarding. But attorneys who are plagued by poor spelling and punctuation have also suffered the Bench's wrath. The Minnesota Supreme

Court listed spelling among the factors warranting one attorney's public reprimand,[79] and Judge Robert Gettleman of Illinois' Northern District once observed that poor spelling makes a brief appear "sloppy."[80]

Benchslaps for spelling can be subtle. Senior Judge John L. Kane of the District of Colorado noted that plaintiff's pleadings were "replete with misspellings, grammatical aberrations, non sequiturs and solecism," and simply reproduced his favorite error in a footnote: "Exercise of pendant jurisdiction is within trial courts [sic] desecration [sic]."[81] Judge Richard Amerian of California's Second District Court of Appeals similarly embarrassed counsel by quoting in his opinion, without comment, a brief passage from plaintiff's complaint that contained six separate spelling and grammatical errors. He included "[sic]" prominently beside each:

> ... "[T]hey are the first cousins of Ian Glenn McSweaney, with whom they "had a very close emotional attachment **[sic]**." It is further alleged that appellants and McSweaney "played together often and had a relationship analagous **[sic]** to a relationship between siblings. Plaintiffs **[sic]** loved [McSweaney] as they would their own brother."

> Appellants brought this action after sustaining "great emotional distrubance **[sic]** and shock and injury to their nervous system **[sic]**, resulting in gastrointestinal disorders, head aches **[sic]**, shock, anxiety, and loss of sleep..."[82]

Although misspelled words are embarrassing, it is punctuation that can decisively alter the meaning of a document.

Cases, careers and livelihoods have been crushed by the disproportionate power of a misplaced comma.

In *Ward v. Ward*, the court's entire finding regarding a trustee's power hinged on the presence of a single comma.[83] In *Henderson v. State*, discussed above, the lack of a period rendered a criminal indictment nonsensical.[84] And in *People v. Vasquez*, an affidavit was disregarded and a complaint dismissed because a misplaced comma made it unclear whether a key affidavit was hearsay: "It may be that the confusion [about the affidavit] arises from the typographical error of placing a comma before the expression 'upon information and belief.' Had the comma not existed, the entire expression 'and that the assertion upon information and belief' would have referred back to the earlier mentioned accusatory instruments so as to render the affidavit non-hearsay."[85]

Some judges have written at length about poor punctuation. Judge Stanley Sadur of Illinois' Northern District griped in a published opinion about counsel's confusing and apparently deliberate disregard for proper punctuation and grammar:

[T]here is an inherent potential for confusion between "P.M.F. Services, Inc." and "PMF Services." In fact, though none of the litigants seems to have focused on it, Grady's bank account and checks reflect even more—they use "P.M.F. Services" (periods and all). Indeed, the crux of plaintiffs' Complaint is that Grady used the similarity to steal from P.M.F. With callous disregard for the reader, plaintiffs' counsel has done nothing to minimize the confusion in the Complaint and later memoranda. Rather counsel has maximized the confusion by referring indiscriminately to "PMF Services, Inc." and "P.M.F. Services" as well.

Unfortunately, counsel does not stop there. Despite the presence of two plaintiffs and four defendants, the terms "plaintiff" and "defendant" are often used in the singular, leaving the reader to puzzle out which plaintiff or which defendant is referred to. Similarly, the term "defendants" is often used when counsel does not appear to be referring to all the defendants. And the list could go on—counsel uses possessives without apostrophes, leaving the reader to guess whether he intends a singular or plural possessive, etc. Such sloppy pleading and briefing are inexcusable as a matter of courtesy as well as because of their impact on defendants' ability to respond.

This opinion ultimately dismisses the Complaint against Mt. Greenwood Bank and dismisses one count against Northern Trust Company on substantive grounds, but it also contemplates the possibility that counsel may seek to file an amended complaint to cure the many defects. If he does that, counsel would be advised to ensure that the amended complaint is also readable.[86]

> "[C]ounsel would be advised to ensure that the amended complaint is also readable."

Judge Stanley Sadur, USDC,
Northern District of Illinois

The Ohio Court of Appeals took the time to benchslap one of its former clerks for a similar infraction, observing that, "[a]lthough not prejudicial to the appellant and of no effect to our determination, we note that appellant counsel's brief is replete with over fifty examples of mistakes in punctuation, citation and spelling. We note that appellant's counsel is a former judicial clerk with service to this court and is urged to do credit to his former position by applying greater attention to detail in his brief writing and proofreading efforts before the Bench."[87]

Structure and Organization _____

A less obvious but equally important component of good writing is effective organization. In *Duncan v. AT&T*, a defendant's motion to dismiss was granted in part because plaintiff's complaint was so poorly organized as to be "functionally illegible." The court added that its responsibilities "do not include cryptography, especially when the plaintiff is represented by counsel."[88] District Court Judge James Gwin once criticized a Plaintiff for a brief that "does not contain a single heading, is littered with unsupported conclusory allegations, [and] eschews legal analysis for paragraph-long block quotes" – though Judge Gwin was able to "piece together enough of [the] poorly-developed record to address in substance most of … the claim."[89]

In many instances, the broad organizational structure of a pleading is determined by federal, state or local rules of court. For example, California Rule of Court 8.504 dictates the sections to be included in a Petition for Review by the California Supreme Court. Failure to follow a court's organizational rules is a sure way to earn a benchslap. For example, California Superior Court

Judge Stephen Perk benchslapped counsel in the following tentative opinion for failing to structure his motion for summary judgment in compliance with the state's rules of court:

> Plt. fails to meet his burden of proof. Notice is insufficient, failing to comply with CCP 437c(a). No points and Authorities accompanies the motion in violation of CRC 3.1113. No Separate Statement of Undisputed Fact accompanies the motion. CCP 437c. No facts are presented to the court with the motion that even begins to meet the burden of proof required for a summary judgment. The moving papers in the "motion" are nothing short of AWFUL. The form of the motion doesn't come close to complying with the rules of court.[90]

> Judge Steven L. Perk, Orange County Superior Court

———————————————

Good luck explaining that tentative opinion to a client.

Tone

Another critical component of legal writing is appropriate tone. While judges, by virtue of their positions, needn't worry about the tone of their tentative or final dispositions, attorneys are not so lucky. Tone is an important aspect of writing that is often overlooked, particularly by junior attorneys who associate combativeness with effective advocacy. Given that attorneys have been sanctioned and pleadings stricken on account of tone, perhaps junior attorneys should start paying closer attention.

Richard O'Brien, an accomplished lawyer for Chicago-based Sidley Austin, learned this when he was benchslapped during oral argument for his "unbridled sarcasm" in a reply brief he filed with District Court Judge Diane Cannon. "This reply is dripping … with sarcasm," Judge Cannon said. "It's not the law, it's not the facts, it's sarcasm." Judge Cannon demanded to know who wrote the brief, and noting that no attorney's name appeared on the pleading,[iv] stated that, "If you want to editorialize … you have to put your name on it." She refused to proceed with the scheduled hearing.[91]

Even if Mr. O'Brien's brief contained more substance than it was credited by Judge Cannon, that substance was overshadowed by its dismissive tone. The brief's two opening sentences are illustrative: "The State's response brief evinces a surprising lack of comprehension of the requirements of [the Act] and an equally surprising lack of affinity for the important First Amendment values that underlie the Act and the role of investigative reporting in promoting those values. The State demonstrates its lack of understanding in several ways…" Still, Mr. Cannon's brief is polite compared to some pleadings.

In *U.S. v. Venable*, Judge Allyson K. Duncan of the Fourth Circuit had no patience for a government brief that pushed the boundaries of respect and civility. She called out U.S. attorney Neil MacBride with this lengthy, scathing footnote:

> Finally, we feel compelled to note that advocates, including government lawyers, do themselves a disservice when their briefs contain disrespectful or uncivil language directed against

---

[iv] Mr. O'Brien's name did, in fact, appear on page 14 of the brief.

the district court, the reviewing court, opposing counsel, parties, or witnesses. *See, e.g., Dranow v. United States,* 307 F.2d 545, 549 (Eighth Cir. 1962) ("In light of the too numerous decisions of this and other Courts of Appeals, it should not be necessary for us to repeat, [a] brief should not contain language disrespectful to the court nor to opposing counsel and ordinarily a brief containing such scurrilous and scandalous matter should be stricken from the files." (internal quotations omitted)); 36 C.J.S. Federal Courts § 557 (2011) ("Abusive, scandalous, scurrilous, . . . or disrespectful language . . . should not be inserted in the brief."); 4 C.J.S. Appeal and Error § 734 (2011) ("The appellate brief should not contain disrespectful, scandalous, or abusive language directed against the court of review, trial judge, opposing counsel, or parties or witnesses. A brief in no case can be used as a vehicle for the conveyance of … insult, disrespect or professional discourtesy of any nature … invectives are not argument, and have no place in legal discussion.").

Unfortunately, the government's brief is replete with such language: it disdains the district court's "abrupt handling" of Appellant's first case, Appellee's Br. 19; sarcastically refers to Appellant's previous counsel's "new-found appreciation for defendant's mental abilities," Appellee's Br. 21; criticizes the district court's "oblique language" on an issue unrelated to this appeal, Appellee's Br. 22; states that the district court opinion in Jones "revealed a crabby and complaining reaction to Project Exile," Appellee's Br. 57; insinuates that the district court's concerns "require[ ] a belief in the absurd that is similar in kind to embracing paranormal conspiracy theories," Appellee's Br. 59; and accuses Appellant of being a "charlatan" and "exploit[ing] his identity as an African-American,"

Appellee's Br. 61. The government is reminded that such disrespectful and uncivil language will not be tolerated by this court. *See Ruston v. Dallas County Tex.*, 320 F. App'x. 262, 263 (Fifth Cir. 2009) (striking pleadings because they "contain abusive and disrespectful language"); *Carter v. Daniels*, 91 F. App'x. 83, 84 (Tenth Cir. 2004) (finding party's "language in his brief intemperate and disrespectful of this court and the district court," and cautioning party that it may be subject to sanctions if it continues to file such pleadings); *Hamad v. Desahazo*, 1996 WL 556788, at *1 (Fifth Cir. 1996) (unpublished) (warning party that "the use of abusive and uncivil language, as displayed in his appellate brief, will not be tolerated by this court" and directing him to "review all pending appeals to make sure that they do not contain such language").[92]

Judge Allyson K. Duncan,
Fourth Circuit Court of Appeals

———————————

The above opinions suggest that overblown rhetoric in a brief is not only unpersuasive, it is harmful. Dale Fischer of California's Central District made this same point to counsel during a sanctions hearing:

> ... I also want to tell you, I don't know why lawyers do this, and there's a lot of them in the room so take heed, all of you, language like "failures are staggering, violations of this magnitude rarely occur, stunning display of incompetence, bitter irony, breathtaking dereliction of duty" are not only

unpersuasive, they're somewhat annoying. I don't have time for rhetoric. I'm really, really busy…

I don't know whether you stay up nights trying to think of clever phrases, but trust me, no judge that I've ever spoken to has ever said, "Boy, can that guy turn a phrase." They only say, "Boy, why didn't he get to the point?" So, please, in future pleadings, remember that.

> Judge Dale Fischer, USDC,
> Central District of California

———————————————

Counsel should also remember that tone is conveyed not just in words and phrasing, but in presentation. Attorneys who submit pleadings or correspondence that adopt too familiar a tone or fail to observe legal formalities may find themselves on the receiving end of a benchslap. Consider the following pithy benchslap from District Court Judge Lynn Hughes.

1. Motions to the court must be filed with a caption.
2. E-mails will not be read and will be deleted. The court is not your ex-girlfriend's Facebook wall.[93]

> Judge Lynn N. Hughes, USDC,
> Southern District of Texas

———————————————

This was not the first time Judge Hughes issued a similar admonishment. Just six months earlier he reminded counsel in a patent case that "the court is not an ex-girlfriend's Facebook wall. All documents must be filed with the court, captioned, signed by counsel, and with service certified."[94] Attorneys who come of age in a digital era of e-mails, texts and tweets may find it difficult to operate in a world of paper pleadings and complete sentences. But as Judge Sparks once remarked, "pleadings filed in the United States District Courts are not press releases, internet blogs, or pieces of investigative journalism."[95] Counsel should remember that many judges and attorneys still demand a certain degree of formality with respect to pleadings, correspondence and appearances.

Legal Citations

Perhaps the most complicated component of legal writing is integrating relevant and accurate citations into a brief. What citations to use, how to use them and how to make them work seamlessly within a legal document is a skill that develops only with experience, and sometimes not at all. Nonetheless, very few benchslaps are delivered for clumsy citations. The majority of citation smack downs are for failing to use citations *at all* or, even worse, for using inaccurate citations.

Citation infractions may not always be premeditated. This is because some attorneys write legal briefs backwards; rather than researching first and writing later, they draft documents blindly and then hunt law to support optimistic arguments. If the actual law is not forthcoming, those attorneys must decide whether to advance their arguments despite no legal authority or to cite inapplicable case law to give an illusion of authority. Many junior attorneys have been sent on wild goose chases by senior attorneys to find case law that simply doesn't exist.

In *In re Shepperson*, a Vermont attorney submitted multiple briefs to the state's courts during a seven-year period that "[made] numerous citation errors that made identification of cases difficult, cited cases for irrelevant or incomprehensible reasons, made legal arguments without citation to authority, and inaccurately represented the law contained in the cited cases." One brief, more than 90 pages long, "fail[ed] to raise a legitimate legal issue or cite a single authority in support of his arguments."[96] In *Espitia v. Fouche*, a case before the Wisconsin Court of Appeals, counsel was fined $100 for an incorrect footnote and issued the following benchslap:

> Counsel for Espitia cites to an unpublished case assertedly upholding a stipulated damages clause due to the difficulty of ascertaining "the exact amount of income certain vending machines would produce." The cite provided is "*Buellesbach v. Roob*, 2005 AP 160 (Ct.App.Dist.I)." *Buellesbach* indeed is unpublished but it has nothing to do with liquidated damage clauses or vending machines; it is a misrepresentation case brought by newlyweds against a wedding photographer. Also, "2005 AP 160" is the docket number, which we discovered only after reaching a dead end at 2005 WI App 160, 285 Wis.2d 472, 702 N.W.2d 433. At last we located the unpublished case that addresses the subject matter for which counsel cited *Buellesbach*:

"Different name, different citation, different district but, as promised, unpublished."

Stansfield Vending, Inc. v. Osseo Truck Travel Plaza, LLC, 2003 WI App 201, 267 Wis.2d 280, 670 N.W.2d 558. Different name, different citation, different district (District IV) but, as promised, unpublished. It is a violation of Wis. Stat. Rule 809.19(1)(e) to provide citations which do not conform to the Uniform System of Citation and of Wis. Stat. Rule 809.23(3) to cite to unpublished opinions. One reason may be that they can be time-consuming to locate. A $100 penalty is imposed against Espitia's counsel. *See Hagen v. Gulrud*, 151 Wis.2d 1, 8, 442 N.W.2d 570 (Ct.App.1989).[97]

Judge C.J. Anderson, Wisconsin Court of Appeals

———————————

Aside from the more fundamental problem of failing to cite legal authority, some attorneys identify proper authority but simply format the citation incorrectly. Incorrectly formatted citations annoy judges because they make it difficult for them to find a case and determine applicable law. For example, an Arizona court admonished counsel to adhere to Bluebook citation form so that lawyers and others could follow the citations,[98] and a Vermont court criticized an appellant's brief that was "riddled with inaccurate and incomplete case citations" and lacked point cites.[99] In *Cook v. Hilltown Township*, the court noted that "the carelessness manifested by inaccurate citations is not in keeping with the tradition of the legal profession," adding that a traditional hallmark of "an outstanding legal brief [is] the accuracy of its citations."[100] When citation errors are egregious and prevalent, they render a brief unhelpful to the court and damaging to the advocate.

Staple Carefully

Even if a pleading is well-written, consider its packaging. New York Justice Charles J. Markey may have denied a motion for summary judgment in part because it was stapled so negligently that it caused physical injury to all who handled it. Although the court's order observes that the motion wasn't signed by counsel, lacked a required affidavit and was otherwise deficient, Justice Markey also noted prominently in his order that "poor stapling of the papers was so negligent as to inflict, and did inflict repeatedly, physical injury to the court personnel handling them."[v] He added, "Such negligence on the part of counsel shows a lack of consideration."[101]

New York attorney Jeffrey Hirsch was asked about the incident by the New York Law Journal and observed that in the more than 5,000 cases he has handled the court had never previously criticized his or his assistants' stapling skills.[102] On the other hand, a spokesperson for the judge said that the staple contributing to dismissal was dangerous enough to draw blood. Twice.

The Perfect Storm

Individually, any of the issues above is problematic. When combined, they create a perfect storm of writing errors

---

[v] Justice Markey later denied that stapling played a role in the dismissal.

that can elicit judicial hysterics. In *Stanard v. Nygren*, attorney Walter Maksym represented a property owner who alleged the county sheriff was forcing his client to hire deputies for special events. Mr. Maksym attempted to file his complaint three times in federal court, and three times his complaint was rejected for failure to state a claim. After the county's third successful motion to dismiss, the trial court dismissed the claim without leave to amend.

Mr. Maksym, having never read this book or its warnings regarding the Seventh Circuit, appealed the dismissal. The resulting benchslap from Judge Diane Sykes is one he will never forget.

We affirm. The district court was well within its discretion to reject the second amended complaint and dismiss the case with prejudice. Each iteration of the complaint was generally incomprehensible and riddled with errors, making it impossible for the defendants to know what wrongs they were accused of committing. Maksym's persistent failure to comply with basic directions from the court and his open defiance of court orders amply justified the judge's decision to dismiss with prejudice. Moreover, like his pleadings in the district court, Maksym's appellate briefing is woefully deficient, raising serious concerns about his competence to practice before this court. Accordingly, we order Maksym to show cause why he should not be suspended from the bar of this court or otherwise disciplined under Rule 46 of the Federal Rules of

> "[Counsel]'s appellate briefing is woefully deficient, raising serious concerns about his competence to practice before this court."

Appellate Procedure. Finally, we direct the clerk to send a copy of this opinion to the Illinois Attorney Registration and Disciplinary Commission.

We describe the facts only briefly and as best we can decipher them from the second amended complaint and Stanard's appellate briefs. The procedural history of the case is also important to the resolution of the issues on appeal...

The defendants moved for a more definite statement under Rule 12(e) of the Federal Rules of Civil Procedure. Stanard was ordered to either respond or file a notice saying that he declined to do so. Maksym ignored the motion and order. Nevertheless, a magistrate judge denied Rule 12(e) relief. Nygren then moved to dismiss the official-capacity claims. Maksym continued to disregard deadlines. Stanard's response to Nygren's motion was due in October 2007, but Maksym failed to respond. Three months later, the court, on its own motion, extended this deadline to February 11, but again Maksym failed to respond by that date. On February 19 he finally filed a response to Nygren's motion.

In the meantime, the defendants jointly moved to dismiss the rest of the complaint pursuant to Rule 12(b)(6) of the Federal Rules of Civil Procedure. The court set a January 11, 2008 deadline for Stanard to respond. Maksym missed this deadline, too. On January 23, nearly two weeks after the deadline to respond had expired, Maksym asked for an extension of time. The court granted this request and extended the deadline to March 18. On June 18, three months after the extended deadline, the district court extended the deadline *again* and ordered a response by July 2. The court's June 18 order warned Maksym that if he failed to timely respond, Stanard's case would be dismissed for want of prosecution under Rule 41(b) of the Federal Rules of Civil Procedure. Maksym filed his response on July 2.

The district court granted the motions to dismiss. The court dismissed the frivolous claims mentioned above [and] held that the rest of the complaint suffered from serious deficiencies under Rules 8(a)(2) (requiring a "short and plain statement" of the claims), 8(d)(1) (requiring pleading to be "simple, concise, and direct"), and 10(b) (requiring claims to be set forth in separate paragraphs and limited to single sets of circumstances "as far as practicable"). The court dismissed the remaining 25 claims without prejudice and gave Maksym until September 30, 2008, to cure the complaint's deficiencies. Helpfully, the court included a list of errors that needed to be fixed.

At *10:34 p.m.* on September 30, Maksym moved for an extension of time to file his amended complaint. The stated basis for this motion was that Maksym's computer was damaged in an earthquake while he was in California sitting for that state's bar exam *in late July.* [Footnote 5: The motion recounted Maksym's strenuous efforts to get the computer fixed. He said he visited Apple "Genius" teams in both Los Angeles and Chicago and took the computer to a "Macspecialist." Though these efforts eventually resolved the immediate problem, he claimed that intermittent data losses persisted.] Maksym also alleged that he

> "He said he visited Apple 'Genius' teams in both Los Angeles and Chicago and took the computer to a 'Macspecialist.'"

was suffering from bilateral carpal tunnel syndrome, severe back and hip pain, and a serious infection. Over the defendants' objection, the court granted the motion and set a new due date of October 22 at 5 p.m. At *4:59 p.m.* on October 22, Maksym filed a motion for leave to file his amended complaint; the amended complaint itself was not filed until 7:01 p.m. that day. His attempt to cure the deficiencies in the original complaint was haphazard at best. Some of the counts were completely unchanged, and many of the specific concerns raised by the district court were not adequately addressed. The court denied leave to file the amended complaint. Rather than dismissing the case with prejudice, however, the court gave Maksym one more opportunity to submit a proper complaint, setting a deadline of October 31 at 5 p.m.

On October 31, at 4:41 p.m., Maksym filed another motion for leave to amend, along with a second amended complaint inexplicably titled "First Amended Complaint." Again, few of the many errors in the earlier complaints were fixed. The district court rejected Maksym's latest effort, outlining at length the many pleading defects in the second amended complaint. To illustrate its basic incoherence, the court quoted verbatim from a number of its paragraphs, including one that contained a staggering and incomprehensible 345–word sentence. The court also took note of the "grammatical and spelling errors" throughout the complaint, which it said were "too numerous to add '[sic]' where required." Noting that the purpose of Rules 8 and 10 is to provide "'fair notice' of the claims and the grounds upon which the claims rest," the court held that the second amended complaint was "so poorly drafted and obviously not in compliance with" the rules of pleading that the defendants were left to "guess which actions apply to each claim." Rather than give Maksym yet another opportunity to replead, by this time the court had had enough:

> Based on the lack of diligence, including a pattern of waiting until the last minute (sometimes literally) to file their motions to amend with non-compl[ia]nt proposed amended complaints attached, the failure to comply with this court's previous orders, and this court's explicit warning of the consequences for doing so, plaintiffs will not be afforded another opportunity to replead.

Accordingly, the court dismissed the federal claims with prejudice and relinquished jurisdiction over the supplemental state-law claims.

Maksym's inability to articulate a "short and plain statement" of his clients' claims for relief did not end in the district court, nor did he improve his approach to court-ordered deadlines and following simple directions once the case reached this court. Maksym sought and received no fewer than three extensions of time to file his opening brief on appeal. [Footnote 6: Each of these extensions was requested based on some combination of health issues, computer troubles, and pressing deadlines in other cases.] Along the way we admonished him for filing his extension motions late and failing to comply with Circuit Rule 26, which requires specificity in motions to extend time. Even with three extensions, Maksym was unable to file his brief on time.

> "Even with three extensions, [Counsel] was unable to file his brief on time."

Instead, he filed his opening brief four days *after* the third extended deadline came and went, including with it an instanter motion seeking leave to file the brief late. Maksym claimed in the motion that he had mailed the brief to the defendants on the due date (he included FedEx receipts), but said he encountered some duplication problems that prevented him from timely filing the brief with the court. Over the defendants' objection, we accepted the late brief. We later ordered it stricken for failure to contain a jurisdictional statement that complies with Rule 28(a)(4)(C) of the Federal Rules of Appellate Procedure. Maksym subsequently submitted a corrected brief…

Though length alone is generally insufficient to justify rejecting a complaint, unintelligibility is certainly a legitimate reason for doing so. Again, the issue is notice; where the lack of organization and basic coherence renders a complaint too confusing to determine the facts that constitute the alleged wrongful conduct, dismissal is an appropriate remedy. In *Garst* we affirmed the dismissal of a 155–page, 400–paragraph complaint that would have forced the defendants to spend countless hours "fishing" for the few relevant allegations:

[E]ven if it were possible to navigate through these papers to a few specific instances of fraud, why should the court be obliged to try? Rule 8(a) requires parties to make their pleadings straightforward, so that judges and adverse parties need not try to fish a gold coin from a bucket of mud. Federal judges have better things to do, and the substantial subsidy of litigation (court costs do not begin to cover the expense of the judiciary) should be targeted on those litigants who take the preliminary steps to assemble a comprehensible claim. Garst's lawyer filed documents so long, so disorganized, so laden with cross-references and baffling acronyms, that they could not alert either the district judge or the defendants to the principal contested matters. *Id.; see also Davis,* 269 F.3d at 820 ("The dismissal of a complaint on the ground that it is unintelligible is unexceptionable.").

Applying these principles here, the district court was well within its discretion in refusing to accept Stanard's proposed second amended complaint. We agree that it crossed the line from just "unnecessarily long" to "unintelligible." Though the complaint was far longer than it needed to be, prolixity was not its chief deficiency. Rather, its rampant grammatical, syntactical, and typographical errors contributed to an overall sense of unintelligibility. This was compounded by a vague, confusing, and conclusory articulation of the factual and legal basis for the claims and a general "kitchen sink" approach to pleading the case. This was Maksym's third attempt to draft a comprehensible pleading, yet his effort to comply with the court's earlier directions was half-hearted at best; the proffered second amended complaint was rife with errors. We include a sampling to provide an understanding of its shortcomings:

> "[The brief's] rampant grammatical, syntactical, and typographical errors contributed to an overall sense of unintelligibility."

• **Lack of punctuation**. At least 23 sentences contained 100 or more words. This includes sentences of 385, 345, and 291 words but does not include sentences set off with multiple subsections. [Footnote 7: We acknowledge the unfortunate reality that poor writing occurs too often in our profession, but

151

Maksym's complaint is far outside the bounds of acceptable legal writing. See, for example, this 345–word sentence. All errors are in the original: "That pursuant to the RICO Act, Defendants extortive activities constituted a Pattern of Racketeering activity and conspiracy involving violations of 1956(a)(1)(B)(ii), and 18 U.S.C. § 1341 (wire fraud—the use of interstate mail or wire facilities, here telephone and facsimile transmissions), or the causing of any of those things promoting unlawful activity), and 18 U.S.C. § 1951 (interference with commerce and extortion by using and threatening to use legitimate governmental powers to obtain an illegitimate objectives under color of official right by wrongful plan, extortion, intimidation and threat of force and/or other unlawful consequence and through fear and misuse of there office to obstruct, hinder, interfere with, and/or affect commerce and the use and enjoyment of Plaintiffs' property and obtaining, as uniformed public officials payment for unwanted services to which they were not entitled by law, attempting to conceal from the United States of America their true and correct income and the nature thereof so obtained from Plaintiffs in order to attempt to evade paying lawful taxes thereon in violation of 26 U.S.C. § 7201, *et seq.*, thereby using the governmental powers with which they have been entrusted to gain personal or illegitimate rewards and payments which they knew or should have known were made and/or obtained in return for the colorable official acts as aforesaid, and knowing that the property involved in a financial transaction represents the proceeds of some form of unlawful activity, conducts or attempts to conduct such a financial transaction which in fact involves the proceeds of specified unlawful activity with the intent to promote the carrying on of specified unlawful activity all in violation of RICO and the other laws set forth herein, *inter alia, as well as* acts chargeable under any of the following provisions of the laws of the State of Illinois 720 ILCS 5/33–3(d) (official misconduct); 720 ILCS 5/12–11 (criminal home invasion); 720 ILCS 5/19–4 (criminal trespass to a residence) 720 ILCS 5/19–4); (theft 720 ILCS 5/16 (a)(1) & (2) by knowingly obtaining or exerting unauthorized and/or through threat control over Plaintiff's property as aforesaid."

• **Near incomprehensibility**. Much of the writing is little more than gibberish. An example:

Stanard and attendees, were stunned on the day of the family-oriented event, when an even more menacing law enforcement presence was created when Nygren's armed deputies, without prior consent or permission, warrant or probable cause, arrived, not a part of any agreement and a surprise and upset when it arrive, uninvited, on and entered and trespassed on Plaintiff property with drug-sniffing 'K–9' dogs, obviously and unfortunate that Defendants were 'looking for trouble' where there was none as distinct from "looking to serve".

• **Failure to follow basic directions**. Given three attempts to file a proper complaint, Maksym could not even bring himself to correct the errors cataloged by the district court following the first two rejections. The district court directed Maksym to separate his facts into sections relevant to each claim rather than just one massive section of "facts common to all counts." Maksym failed to do so. When it came to identifying the claims, conclusory allegations abounded. A few examples: (1) the defendants used wire transmissions to facilitate the scheme; (2) the defendants engaged in a pattern or practice of wrongful behavior; (3) Nygren had decision-making authority for the county; and (4) the defendants' actions implicated interstate commerce because McHenry County is near the Wisconsin border.

• **Failure to put defendants on notice**. Despite the complaint's length—or perhaps in part because of it—it remains unclear what constitutes the core of the claims against Nygren and the other defendants. For example, the § 1983 claim does not allege anything more concrete than that the defendants violated Stanard's First, Fourth, Fifth, and Fourteenth Amendment rights.

• **Grammatical and syntactical errors**. The district court put it best: "The grammatical and spelling errors" are "too numerous to add '[sic]' where required."

Perhaps these defects, considered alone, might not justify the court's rejection of the second amended complaint. Collectively, however, they are easily egregious enough to warrant denial of the motion for leave to amend. The complaint's lack of clarity would have severely disadvantaged the defendants when it came time to responsively plead to, much less defend against, the claims. To form a defense, a defendant must know what he is defending against; that is, he must know the legal wrongs he is alleged to have committed and the factual allegations that form the core of the claims asserted against him. Deciphering even that much from the second amended complaint is next to impossible. To the extent that discerning the basic legal and factual basis of the claims is not impossible but merely unnecessarily difficult, we restate the primary teaching of *Garst:* A federal court is not obligated to sift through a complaint to extract some merit when the attorney who drafted it has failed to do so himself. *See Garst,* 328 F.3d at 378. "Rule 8(a) requires parties to make their pleadings straightforward, so that judges and adverse parties need not try to fish a gold coin from a bucket of mud." *Id.* Maksym failed so thoroughly in this regard that the district court was well within its discretion to deny the motion for leave to amend.

The court's decision to dismiss the case with prejudice was also eminently reasonable. Again, this was Maksym's third attempt to plead properly, and he was still far from doing so. Moreover, Maksym repeatedly failed to follow explicit directions from the district

> "This was [Counsel's] third attempt to plead properly, and he was still far from doing so."

court about how to correct specific problems in the first two complaints. The failures are too numerous to list here, but take as an example Maksym's approach to the § 1983 claim. As we have noted, the first complaint alleged in a wholly conclusory fashion that the defendants had violated Stanard's First, Fourth, Fifth, Eighth, and Fourteenth Amendment rights. Reviewing that complaint, the district court noted that "the allegations in Count III [the § 1983 count] do not permit the court to determine which of the allegations in paragraphs 1–41 ... support the alleged violations of the five constitutional amendments referred to in Count III." The court admonished Maksym "to be mindful of his obligation ... to ensure that any claims asserted are warranted by existing law or by a nonfrivolous argument for extending, modifying, or reversing existing law or for establishing new law." The court issued this reminder "in light of the fact that the current complaint contain[s] several questionable claims," noting in particular that it purported to assert a violation of the Eighth Amendment, which protects only those who have been convicted of a crime. *See Lewis v. Downey*, 581 F.3d 467, 474 (Seventh Cir.2009).

Rather than fix these and other errors identified by the court, Maksym submitted a proposed amended complaint that in most respects used exactly the same language, even reasserting the frivolous Eighth Amendment claim. As the district court noted, plaintiffs have made no attempt to cure the problems with the § 1983 based claims.... In fact, but for the adjustment of paragraph numbers, these claims are unchanged and remain deficient for the reasons stated in [the court's previous order].... Moreover, plaintiffs' counsel has failed to heed the court's warning to remain mindful of his obligations under Rule 11 by continuing to allege a violation of the Eighth Amendment without any facts demonstrating the plausibility of such a claim. Failure to comply with Rule 11 may result in sanctions.

Maksym was then given a third opportunity to plead correctly despite his flagrant disregard for the court's first order. He continued to demonstrate either an inability or unwillingness to comply with basic directions. Although Maksym removed the reference to the Eighth Amendment in the § 1983 claim, he made no other legitimate effort to comply with the court's directives. In the district court's words, Maksym's latest amendment did "nothing to correct the deficiencies previously identified. The court and defense counsel remain in the dark as to which acts ... by which defendants violated which of the four constitutional provisions that plaintiffs allege were transgressed."

It is true that the pleading rules favor decisions on the merits rather than technicalities, *see Foman,* 371 U.S. at 182, 83 S.Ct. 227, and also that leave to amend pleadings should be freely given, FED.R.CIV.P. 15(a)(2) ("The court should freely give leave [to amend] when justice so requires."). But these general principles have some limits. Leave to replead need not be allowed in cases of "repeated failure to cure deficiencies by amendments previously allowed." *Foman,* 371 U.S. at 182, 83 S.Ct. 227. We have shown considerable deference to the informed judgments of district judges who must decide whether to dismiss a case with prejudice when counsel repeatedly fails to plead properly. For example, we affirmed a district court's decision to dismiss with prejudice after giving counsel four opportunities over four years to file a proper complaint. *Airborne Beepers & Video, Inc. v. AT & T Mobility LLC,* 499 F.3d 663, 668 (Seventh Cir.2007). In *Airborne Beepers* the district court had provided concrete instructions about how to fix the defects in each successive version of the complaint, and still counsel failed to do so. *Id.* at 665–66.

The same is true here. Maksym had three opportunities to file a complaint that complied with the rules, yet he failed to follow basic instructions from the court. In many ways Maksym's conduct was much more egregious than that of the attorneys in *Airborne Beepers.* There, plaintiff's counsel at least had made concrete changes to the complaint at each stage in an effort to comply with the court's directions. Here, in contrast, Maksym made almost no changes in each new version of his complaint. As such, he flagrantly disobeyed the court's patient instructions. Moreover, he missed multiple deadlines and barely made others that had been repeatedly extended. The record as a whole attests to the district court's diligence in attempting to move the case past the pleadings stage; yet despite the court's earnest efforts, Maksym did not take advantage of the repeated opportunities he was given. Under the circumstances, the judge was fully justified in not giving him another chance. *See Frederiksen v. City of Lockport*, 384 F.3d 437, 439 (Seventh Cir.2004) (dismissal with prejudice was appropriate where plaintiff failed to comply with Rule 10(b) over multiple attempts and years and where district court reasonably viewed failure to comply as defiance of court orders). The principle that leave to amend should be freely granted does not require district judges to repeatedly indulge attorneys who show little ability or inclination to comply with the rules. *Cf. Atkins v. City of Chicago,* 631 F.3d 823, 832 (Seventh Cir.2011) ("The plaintiff's lawyer has had four bites at the apple. Enough is enough.").

One final note: Compounding the problems he exhibited in the district court, Maksym failed to file a reasonably coherent brief on appeal. All the deficiencies that plagued the

> "[Counsel] failed to file a reasonably coherent brief on appeal."

various versions of the complaint also infected his briefs here. Maksym never directly addressed the issues before this court, relying instead on cases of marginal or no relevance. In the table of authorities in his opening brief, he cites 81 cases, but almost all of them are completely irrelevant to the issues presented here. In his reply brief, after the defendants had crystallized the issues, Maksym again failed to meaningfully— or even comprehensibly—articulate an argument. His appellate briefing was characterized by a reliance on irrelevant, conclusory, and often incoherent arguments of which the following is a representative example: "Plaintiffs claims were not 'intelligible'—no 'needle in a haystack' as Appellees' claim."

In short, Maksym's entire approach to this case was alarmingly deficient. For all the foregoing reasons, we hold that the district court was well within its discretion to deny leave to file the second amended complaint and to dismiss the case with prejudice. We also order Maksym to show cause within 21 days why he should not be removed or suspended from the bar of this court or otherwise disciplined under Rule 46(b) or (c) of the Federal Rules of Appellate Procedure. We also direct the clerk of this court to send a copy of this opinion to the Attorney Registration and Disciplinary Commission of Illinois for any action it deems appropriate.[103]

Judge Diane Sykes, Seventh Circuit

A Public Outcry

If judicial ridicule and referral to the state bar isn't sufficient motivation for attorneys to become skilled copy editors, than perhaps peer pressure is. For better or worse, attorneys appear increasingly willing to issue public criticism against their colleagues. Meanwhile, legal bloggers circle like sharks to provide a forum to view attorneys humbled for poor writing.

Case-in-point is attorney Anissa Bluebaum, who drafted a complaint on behalf of a convicted sex offender who filed a civil suit against her probation officer. The pleading contained a number of grammatical errors that made it difficult to understand. Rather than meet and confer regarding this issue, opposing counsel Richard D. Crites filed an excoriating "Motion to Clarify" that labeled the complaint "the worst example of pleading that the defendant's attorney has ever witnessed or read."[104]

The primary source of Mr. Crites' dissatisfaction was Ms. Bluebaum's inconsistent use of apostrophes. He writes in his motion that "Defendant does not know whether plaintiff is just not familiar with the use of possessives or whether plaintiff was referring to merely one of the defendants … is this merely the poor usage of the English language by plaintiff's attorney? We have no earthly idea which is the case."[105]

The blogosphere picked up on Mr. Crites' motion and Ms. Bluebaum became a symbol for lawyers across the country who are fed up with poorly written pleadings. The comments about her and her work product were, to say the least, unkind. Newspaper articles followed her story and noted that Ms. Bluebaum had, just weeks earlier, been criticized in open court by Judge Calvin Holden, who threatened to hold her in contempt and reminded her that she went to law school and knew how an attorney should behave.[106]

The pleading and subsequent criticism must have been crushing. While at least one newspaper account references a "letter of response" from Ms. Bluebaum, that letter was not filed with the court and this author could find no record of the letter online.[107] However, according to the case docket, Ms. Bluebaum did not clarify her original complaint or file an amended complaint.[108] The case was dismissed on November 8, 2011 for failure to prosecute.[109]

The story of Ms. Bluebaum, whose work product is no worse than that being submitted every day by many attorneys across the country, should serve as a warning to young attorneys: invest in developing and honing legal writing skills. Judges, attorneys and websites are ever eager to crown the next Anissa Bluebaum.

CHAPTER 7: Extreme Incompetence

The attorneys described in chapters 5 and 6 violated rules or submitted poor work product, but those errors may have been isolated mistakes. The same cannot be said of the lawyers described below. Sometimes a lawyer's representation is so troubling that it undermines the very foundation of an adversarial legal system. In these circumstances, judges are prone to take swift action.

In the wake of a blistering benchslap for incompetence, a Vermont court forced attorney Carlyle Shepperson to sign a stipulation with the Vermont Professional Conduct Board to seek tutoring "to develop skills in legal analysis, persuasive writing techniques, writing organization, and use of legal authority, proper citation form, and proper formatting for memoranda and briefs."[110] When Mr. Shepperson failed to obtain the tutoring, he was suspended until he could demonstrate his fitness to practice law. Illinois Justice Joseph Goldenhersh took a similar approach with attorney John Hogan, who "lacked the fundamental skill of drafting pleadings and briefs."[111] Mr. Hogan was placed on inactive bar status until he developed a tutoring plan to remedy his lack of skill. There is no shortage of similar orders from state court judges frustrated by inept counsel.

If state courts have little tolerance for incompetence, federal courts have none at all – particularly not the benchslap factory known as the Seventh Circuit. Chief Judge Frank Easterbook was so appalled by the performance of attorney Michael J. Greco, who was not even licensed to appear before the Court, that he called Mr. Greco a "menace to his clients and a scofflaw with respect to appellate procedure." The accompanying benchslap is devastating.

> …This litigation has gone off the rails because of multiple errors. The failure of Michael J. Greco, representing these three plaintiffs, to act promptly after Judge Castillo's order, is only one problem. It is a fatal one, as we explain below, but Judge Castillo should not have presented Greco with the opportunity to bungle his clients' cases away…

> [O]n the very date that Judge Castillo dismissed the original suit, nominally without prejudice, it was already too late for plaintiffs to file individual suits. They should have appealed immediately. Although a dismissal without prejudice nominally is not final, and thus can't be appealed, when the decision effectively precludes re-filing—as it did here—it is treated as final and appealable. *Schering-Plough Healthcare Products, Inc. v. Schwartz Pharma, Inc.*, 586 F.3d 500, 507 (Seventh Cir. 2009).

An appeal would have produced a remand with instructions to reinstate the suit in compliance with Rules 20(b) and 21. But Greco did not appeal, the time to do so has long passed, and the fact that an un-appealed order dismissing a suit may have been erroneous does not extend the time to file a replacement suit.

Greco does not contend in this court that his suits are timely under §2000e-5(f)(1). Instead he argues that Judge Castillo extended the statute of limitations by granting extra time to file replacement actions. He does not contend that these orders were valid, and they weren't. District judges lack authority to extend statutory periods of limitations. A district judge can't say something like: "The statute gives a plaintiff 90 days to sue, but this is too short, so I am extending the time to 14 months." A statute of limitations confers rights on putative defendants; judges cannot deprive those persons of entitlements under a statute. If a judge can't extend the period of limitations directly, why should orders adding time to re-file a dismissed action be effective?

Perhaps Greco is invoking the idea that a filing with a federal judge may be deemed timely "where a party has performed an act which, if properly done, would [meet] the deadline . . . and has received specific assurance by a judicial officer that this act has been properly done." *Osterneck v. Ernst & Whinney*, 489 U.S. 169, 179 (1989). (This approach no longer affects the time to file notices of appeal. *See Bowles v. Russell*, 511 U.S. 205 (2007); we need not decide its status as applied to non-jurisdictional time limits.) Judge Castillo did not specifically assure Greco that filing new complaints by May 2009 would be "properly done," and thus induce Greco to wait. To the contrary, Judge Castillo set several earlier deadlines, which Greco missed. The timeline is a bit more complex than we have given it, but Greco concedes that he missed the initial deadline set by the district court. By May 2009 the window had long closed; Greco had taken almost five times the statutory limit of 90 days.

It does not help to invoke the doctrine of equitable tolling. A litigant is entitled to equitable tolling if "he shows '(1) that he has been pursuing his rights diligently, and (2) that some extraordinary circumstance stood in his way' and prevented timely filing." *Holland v. Florida*, 130 S. Ct. 2549, 2562 (2010), quoting from *Pace v. DiGuglielmo*, 544 U.S. 408, 418 (2005). Greco did not pursue his clients' rights diligently—after the suit was dismissed in September 2008, effective re-filing took almost three times the 90 days allowed for an initial filing—nor was dismissal without prejudice an "extraordinary circumstance" that undermined his clients' rights. Nothing prevented plaintiffs from appealing Judge Castillo's order dismissing the initial suit, or from filing new suits within the 40 days he set for that task. Greco has never said why he did not meet that deadline. A lawyer's ineptitude does not support equitable tolling. *Lawrence v. Florida*, 549 U.S. 327, 336 (2007). The remedy is not continued litigation against defendants, who are entitled to stand on their right to dismissal when the plaintiff does not file a timely suit; the remedy is a malpractice action against the lawyer whose negligence is responsible for the problem.

> "Greco's calamitous handling of this litigation in the district court has been followed by a sloppy performance in this court."

See, e.g., Farzana K. v. Indiana Department of Education, 473 F.3d 703, 706 (Seventh Cir. 2007) …

Greco's calamitous handling of this litigation in the district court has been followed by a sloppy performance in this court. As we've mentioned, Greco has never related why he did not appeal in September 2008 or file new suits by the end of October 2008. And his performance has been marked by procedural gaffes, three of which led to orders to show cause why the appeal should not be dismissed—and one of which led to his clients' brief being struck.

Circuit Rule 3(c) requires counsel to file a docketing statement within a week of the appeal. Greco failed to file a statement until two weeks after we ordered him to show cause why his inaction should not lead to sanctions. We issued another order in June 2010 directing Greco to reply to a motion to consolidate the three appeals; he ignored our order until we issued a second order to show cause. Then the time for him to file a brief expired; eight days after the deadline, Greco finally submitted a brief, together with a request for a retroactive extension, even though Circuit Rule 26 requires motions for extra time to be filed at least a week before the due date. The belatedly tendered brief did not include a digital version, despite Circuit Rule 31(e). Personnel in the clerk's office called Greco repeatedly; he did not return their calls. This led to the third order to show cause, which at last prodded Greco to submit a digital version—but the version he submitted did not comply with the rule, because it was missing some sections.

Exasperated, we struck the brief but offered to reinstate it if Greco at last complied fully with Circuit Rule 31(e). This order also directed Greco to show cause why he should not be fined or otherwise disciplined for ignoring the inquiries from the clerk's office and failing to comply with Rule 31(e) despite repeated requests.

Greco's response to this last show-cause order, the fourth in a single appeal, is consistent with his performance throughout the litigation. It slights one of the two subjects we directed him to address and does not tell us why he failed to return calls from the clerk's office and disregarded Rule 31(e) until the third show-cause order was issued. (He does say that "Greco has not ignored telephone calls from this court", which essentially accuses the staff of the clerk's office of lying about trying to reach him. We think that unlikely.) And with respect to the subject that it does address, Greco labels his deficient compliance an "oversight" but does not explain why the error was made. We do not penalize lawyers who rely on plausible misreadings of ambiguous rules, but Greco does not contend that Rule 31(e) is ambiguous or offer any explanation for his failure to do what it commands. *Cf. Pioneer Investment Services Co. v. Brunswick Associates Ltd. Partnership*, 507 U.S. 380 (1993).

The events recounted in this opinion show that Greco is a menace to his clients and a scofflaw with respect to appellate procedure. The district court may wish to consider whether he should remain a member of its bar. Would-be clients should

> "[Greco] essentially accuses the staff of the clerk's office of lying about trying to reach him. We think that unlikely."

consider how Greco has treated Lee, Washington, and Moore. Greco has not asked for a hearing on the disciplinary order to show cause, and we now conclude that he has comported himself unprofessionally. We reprimand Greco for this unprofessional behavior and fine him $5,000, payable to the Clerk within 14 days. Greco must send Lee, Washington, and Moore copies of this opinion so that they may consider whether to file malpractice suits against him.

One other observation. Greco was allowed to file briefs and deliver the oral argument on behalf of his clients only as a result of an oversight. He is not a member of this court's bar. Circuit Rule 46(a) gives counsel 30 days after the appeal is docketed to join our bar, if they are not members already. Greco did not meet that deadline and did not even file an application until the appeal was well under way. Ruling on the application was complicated by the fact that Greco was recently disciplined by a state court. Applications that reveal a disciplinary history are subjected to special scrutiny. We will defer action on Greco's application until he has paid the fine. After paying, Greco must submit an affidavit establishing that he is in good standing at all bars to which he has ever been admitted.

> "Greco was allowed to file briefs and deliver the oral argument... only as a result of an oversight. He is not a member of this court's bar."

The judgment is affirmed, sanctions are imposed, and directions are issued.[112]

Chief Judge Frank Easterbrook, Seventh Circuit

_____

Of course, Judge Easterbrook's opinion hasn't slowed Mr. Greco. He maintains an active practice in Chicago and even developed a new website in 2011.[113] Readers can follow him on his recently launched Twitter feed @MichaelGreco18.[114] When contacted about this matter by the ABA Journal in 2009, Mr. Greco replied that he "could not comment."[115]

Like the Seventh Circuit, the Fifth Circuit has little tolerance for inept representation. In an opinion otherwise devoted to the merits of an appeal of a Title VII claim, Judges Carolyn King, Carl Stewart and Edward Prado devoted an entire section to attorney Roger Phipps, who "tried not to read that many cases" and was woefully unprepared for oral argument.

E. Roger Phipps Conduct

Finally, and completely separate and apart from the issues raised on appeal, we would be remiss if we did not comment on the conduct of Roger Phipps, counsel for Hartz, during oral argument in this case on Tuesday, March 4, 2008. Phipps' conduct towards the Court during argument was unprofessional. Even more serious was his admission that during his work on the case (including his preparation for argument), he had not read a key Supreme Court case. His cavalier disregard for his client's interest and for his obligation to the Court was both troubling and disgraceful.

Accordingly, we are ordering Phipps to provide his client, Hartz, a copy of our opinion immediately after it is released. In order to ensure compliance, we are further directing him to supply our Court with proof of service.

The Fifth Circuit included a portion of the trial court transcript in a footnote detailing Mr. Phipps' courtroom misconduct:

Phipps: . . . so that's about all I have to say, Your Honor. I don't have anything other than that. You know, my client lives in Chicago. ... She continues to earn a living, and she's generally unavailable if you call her because she, she's sort of a traveling doctor.

Judge: That's not much of a thing you come in here and tell us, I guess.

Phipps: Well, my attitude is, the [district court] judge got it right . . . . And as far as whether even *Ricks* should apply, I don't think it should.

Judge: What do you do about *Morgan*?

Phipps: I don't, I don't, I don't know *Morgan*, Your Honor.

Judge: You don't know *Morgan*?

Phipps: Nope.

Judge: You haven't read it?

Phipps: I try not to read that many cases, your Honor. *Ricks* is the only one I read. Oh, *Ledbetter*, I read *Ledbetter*, and I read that one that they brought up last night. I don't know if that's not *Ledbetter*, I can't remember the name of it. *Ricks* is the one that I go by; it's my North star. Either it applies or it doesn't apply. I don't think it applies.

Judge: I must say, *Morgan* is a case that is directly relevant to this case. And for you representing the Plaintiff to get up here—it's a Supreme Court case—and say you haven't read it. Where did they teach you that?

170

Phipps: They didn't teach me much, Your Honor.

Judge: At Tulane, is it?

Phipps: Loyola.

Judge: Okay. Well, I must say, that may be an all[-]time first.

Phipps: That's why I wore a suit today, Your Honor.

Judge: Alright. We've got your attitude, anyway.[116]

Judges Carolyn King, Carl Stewart and
Edward Prado, Fifth Circuit

———————————

In the wake of Mr. Phipps' benchslap, there was a scramble by the various "Loyola" law schools scattered across the country to disassociate themselves from the unfortunate litigator. Shortly after the opinion, Loyola-New Orleans' career services department sent out a mass e-mail with the "GOOD NEWS" that Mr. Phipps was not a graduate.[117] The next day, the registrar at Loyola-Chicago confirmed to Alan Childress of the Legal Profession Blog that Mr. Phipps did not attend its law school, either.[118] At around the same, Loyola-New Orleans retracted its previous statement and was forced to acknowledge Mr. Phipps as a graduate.[119]

In fairness to Mr. Phipps, his greatest mistake may have been failing to respond to the court's reprimand with an appropriate tone. (Had he read this book he may have avoided that particular error). His flippant response that he "tr[ies] not to read that many cases" was likely an attempt at humor, albeit a failed one. Similarly, although attorney Joseph Rakofsky appears to have performed poorly in court and was benchslapped for alleged misconduct, it is his response to that benchslap that makes his case particularly troubling.

Defendant Dontrell Deaner was arrested in late 2008 and charged with murder by the District of Columbia. As he approached trial in April 2011, he retained 2009 Touro Law grad Joseph Rakofsky to represent him. Mr. Deaner had reason to be concerned about Mr. Rakofsky's representation. A recent graduate from a lesser-known law school, Mr. Rakofsky's website profile (now removed) noted that he worked for at least three different firms in the brief time since his graduation (it appears that much of that legal experience was as an intern, not an attorney).[vi] Moreover, Mr. Rakofsky was not licensed to practice law in the District of Columbia and had never tried a case before. He raised this last fact with the jury during his opening statement. Despite these potential red flags, Mr. Deaner's family put his fate in the hands of Mr. Rakofsky.[120]

Mr. Rakofsky's representation did not go as planned. He's reported to have clashed repeatedly with his local defense counsel, attorney Sherlock Grigsby, on how to proceed with the case. And his client, Mr. Deaner, was also displeased. The conflict between Mr. Deaner and Mr. Rakofsky reached the point that they asked the judge to appoint a new attorney mid-trial. In a remarkable move, Judge William Jackson granted the request and

---

[vi] Mr. Rakofsky's website has been preserved online by several legal blogs for educational purposes as an example of a website that violates ethical principles of attorney advertising. The website is available online at http://ivi3.com/whitecollarfirmct.com/about_rakofsky_law_firm.html (last checked 1/30/2013).

declared a mistrial.[121] *The Washington Post* described the hearing this way:

> Judge William Jackson told attorney Joseph Rakofsky during a hearing Friday that he was "astonished" at his performance and at his "not having a good grasp of legal procedures" before dismissing him.
>
> What angered Jackson even more was a filing he received early Friday from an investigator hired by Rakofsky in which the attorney told the investigator via an attached e-mail to "trick" a government witness into testifying in court that she did not see his client at the murder scene.
>
> According to the filing, Rakofsky had fired the investigator and refused to pay him after the investigator refused to carry out his orders with the witness. The filing included an e-mail that the investigator said was from Rakofsky, saying: "Thank you for your help. Please trick the old lady to say that she did not see the shooting or provide information to the lawyers about the shooting." The e-mail came from Rakofsky's e-mail account, which is registered to Rakofsky Law Firm in Freehold, N.J.[122]

Even if Mr. Rakofsky's representation was inept or unethical, the story until this point may simply have been a new lawyer who got in over his head. But this gloating Facebook post, allegedly made by Mr. Rakofsky shortly after the mistrial, transformed the narrative:

It appears Mr. Rakofsky was trying to cast the mistrial as a legal strategy when, in fact, it flowed from his client's desire that he be removed as counsel. Seven of his friends "liked" his post. [123]

Mr. Rakofsky's benchslap and subsequent Facebook post were covered extensively by the legal blogosphere, in part because they played into a broader narrative about the quality of law school graduates from lesser known law schools. Although the spotlight must have been intensely embarrassing, it would have passed in time; there are always more benchslaps in the chamber for hapless attorneys.

But Mr. Rakofsky didn't go into hiding. Instead, he filed a lawsuit against every media source that covered his unflattering story. In a suit dubbed "Rakofsky v. Internet," Mr. Rakofsky sued 81 defendants, including a host of legal bloggers, the Washington Post, Washington City Paper, Allbritton Communications, the American Bar Association, Thompson Reuters and others. In January 2012 he sought to add an additional slate of defendants to his claim, including Google, Yahoo! and Techdirt, for "refus[ing] to preserve certain information in the absence of a formal Court order."[124]

Mr. Rakofsky's Complaint is a bizarre rehashing of the Deaner trial coupled with unflattering allegations about presiding Judge Jackson, the private investigator cited in the judge's courtroom comments, and the reporter present for *The Washington Post*. Mr. Rakofsky posits that Judge Jackson's "anger may have been prompted by the diligence and zeal with which RAKOFSKY conducted his defense in the interest of the client as much as anything else, rather than any shortcoming in RAKOFSKY's knowledge of court procedure ..."[125]

The jury may not agree with Mr. Rakofsky's characterization of his own performance. Scott Greenfield of legal blog Simple Justice alleges he spoke with one of the jurors, Randy, who shared this written recollection of Mr. Rakofsky's courtroom abilities:

> Right now, I am looking at a letter addressed to me from Judge William M. Jackson, thanking me for my jury service on the Deaner trial ... and I feel obliged to set the record straight as just that "insider." Additionally, I'd like to thank the judge for his extreme tolerance of Mr. Rakofsky's antics ... to those of us on the jury, we were stupefied and, having sat on many trials in the past myself, Judge Jackson gave Mr. Rakofsky as much "leash" as was professionally possible. It's Mr. Rakofsky's own fault, and frankly narcissism, that allowed him to "hang" himself with that leash and draw a mistrial.

It was obvious from the opening statements that Mr. Rakofsky was way out of his league and poorly trained for a proper court defense. Whatever momentary empathy any of us on the jury may have felt for Mr. Rakofsky's absolute ineptitude, we were quickly absolved by our knowledge that a young man's entire life was at stake. The absolute amateurish antics

> "Whatever momentary empathy any of us on the jury may have felt for Mr. Rakofsky's absolute ineptitude, we were quickly absolved by our knowledge that a young man's entire life was at stake."

displayed by Mr. Rakofsky were repulsive and oddly narcissistic. He had very little command of the law, and now hearing that Mr. Deaner's family actually hired him is truly upsetting. Most of us assumed that this was a court ordered public defender that may just have been too young and overwhelmed by a huge docket of cases to put together a proper defense.

Additionally, the quotes above from Rakofsky [as well as the Facebook entries] make my stomach absolutely turn. His poor performance was much much more than a lack of training and time… he truly had no grasp for how to handle a proper criminal court trial and it was obvious to EVERYONE in the court that he had trouble even putting a proper thought together, often repeating and repeating himself over and over to the audible gasps from the jury. Now, hearing his responses on facebook, I am truly repulsed that this "attorney" could defend his own actions while he wasted the time of the court, those of us on the jury, the money of DC taxpayers and most importantly jeopardized the life of the person he was defending. It's an absolute travesty and mockery of the fragile system that protects ALL of our rights.[126]

It is easy to understand why Mr. Rakofsky wants to scour his name and this case from the Internet. He noted to the *Washington City Paper* that the controversy "embarrasses the hell out of me."[127] One of the demands Mr. Rakofsky made of the defendants in his lawsuit is that they do not mention his name or use his picture.[128] Unfortunately, as observed by Mr. Greenfield of Simple Justice, the "deeper digging [by bloggers and journalists] is a by-product of Rakofsky's own decision to take a bad situation and make it stupendously worse. From afar, he looked horrible. He looked even worse close-up."[129] The term "Rakofsky Effect" has even made it into the Urban Dictionary, where it is defined as "Infinite pleading amendments as the unintended consequence of suing to censor your critics," e.g., "Rakofsky continually amended, the suit adding new defendants seemingly every time a new individual on the Internet spoke critically of him, which only prompted wider criticism, thus creating a self-perpetuating cycle."[130]

Mr. Rakofsky's lawsuit is still pending, though Defendants have filed numerous Motions to Dismiss and requested sanctions against him. Regardless of the outcome, his very public battle against Judge Jackson, journalists and bloggers has tarnished his reputation with his peers. To add insult to injury, the story did not end well for Mr. Rakofsky's former client, Dontrell Deaner. Mr. Deaner spent many more months in prison as his new attorney developed his case, only to plead guilty just two weeks before his new trial. Mr. Deaner was sentenced to ten years in prison to be followed by five years of probation.[131]

As the Rakofsky case demonstrates, legal incompetence is especially concerning in the criminal context, where defendants' lives and victims' rights are on the line. Mr. Richard Rosario provides yet another sobering example of legal incompetence in criminal defense. Mr. Rosario was convicted of murder in 1996 based on the eyewitness testimony of two witnesses who identified him from a book of police photographs. There was no other evidence linking Mr. Rosario to the crime, the victim or the witnesses. Mr. Rosario also had a plausible alibi placing him out of the state at the time the crime occurred. When he learned he was being sought in connection with a crime, he turned himself in and provided the names of more than a dozen people who could substantiate his alibi.[132]

Despite receiving approval from the judge, Mr. Rosario's court-appointed lawyer failed to interview the majority of his alibi witnesses. Four of those witnesses specifically remembered Mr. Rosario being in Florida on the day of the murder. Second Circuit Judge Chester J. Straub described Mr. Rosario's defense as "a colossal failure" and notes that "Rosario received constitutionally ineffective assistance of counsel." Still, the Second Circuit deferred to the trial court's finding to the contrary. The U.S. Supreme Court denied review of the case and Mr. Rosario is currently serving a 25 year sentence.[vii]

The circumstances in *Wilson v. Wainwright* are equally disturbing. Attorney R. E. Conner's handling of a death penalty appeal was so inadequate that it was deemed incompatible with an adversarial legal system and a threat to "the very foundation of justice":

> Appellate counsel, R.E. Conner, briefed only five issues in the initial brief on the merits. At no time did he raise or discuss any issue relating to the sufficiency of the evidence to support the jury's finding of premeditation in either death. This issue was sufficiently apparent from the cold record that the two dissenting justices raised it in their separate opinions. *Wilson*, 436 So.2d at 912 (Overton, J., dissenting), 913 (McDonald, J., dissenting).

[vii] To their credit, Mr. Rosario's attorneys took full responsibility for failing to interview his alibi witnesses. They also provided candid testimony that would have supported a finding that Mr. Rosario received ineffective assistance of counsel. The trial court declined to make such a finding despite their testimony.

The decision not to raise this issue cannot be excused as mere strategy or allocation of appellate resources. This issue is crucial to the validity of the conviction and goes to the heart of the case. If, in fact, the evidence does not support premeditation, petitioner was improperly convicted of first degree murder and death is an illegal sentence. To have failed to raise so fundamental an issue is far below the range of acceptable appellate performance and must undermine confidence in the fairness and correctness of the outcome.

Additionally, Conner failed to address the propriety of the death penalty as applied in either his initial brief or his reply brief, even though the state raised the issue in its answer brief. After oral argument, this Court ordered Conner to file a supplemental brief addressing the death penalty. The result was a descriptive listing of cases in which this Court had discussed the two aggravating factors in dispute and a passing reference to one possible statutory mitigating circumstance. The application of case law to the facts before the Court was cursory and totally lacking in persuasive advocacy.

> "Any appellate counsel who, after being ordered to address the issue, responds with such an inadequate, unpartisan brief has failed to grasp the vital importance of his role as a champion of his client's cause."

Any appellate counsel who, after being ordered to address the issue, responds with such an inadequate, unpartisan brief has failed to grasp the vital importance of his role as a champion of his client's cause. We do not approve of counsel urging frivolous claims, nor do we require that every colorable claim, regardless of relative merit, be raised on appeal. However, the basic requirement of due process in our adversarial legal system is that a defendant be represented in court, at every level, by an advocate who represents his client zealously within the bounds of the law. Every attorney in Florida has taken an oath to do so and we will not lightly forgive a breach of this professional duty in any case; in a case involving the death penalty it is the very foundation of justice.

At oral argument, Conner also demonstrated lack of preparation and zeal in urging his client's cause.

In the opening moments of oral argument, the following colloquy took place:

THE COURT: ... You don't consider [the legality of the sentence] with any materiality or relevance in a case where ... the death penalty has been imposed, sir?

CONNER: Uh, those particular points about the aggravating and mitigating circumstance, uh, I felt the prior decision of this court were clear that with the aggravating circumstances as found by the court, that and with no mitigating circumstances that it was, uh, in an area where the court had already decided, unless something has changed in the interim...

THE COURT: Well, let me ask a question. Do you feel that death is the appropriate punishment if he is guilty.

CONNER: It's, it's quite possible, yes sir. Uh, there was sufficient evidence in this case for the jury to find premeditation and they did find premeditation.

Later in the argument, the discussion continued:

THE COURT: Would you agree that the evidence concerning the fact of his committing first degree murder in this instance was pretty overwhelming?

CONNER: I would say that it was overwhelming…

THE COURT: May I ask you this please sir. Now, on the one hand, if I'm reading it correctly, you're saying that there is no question about the guilt and then your statement of the guilt there that the death penalty is appropriate. Am I misunderstanding you?

CONNER: No, I don't-I don't think I meant to say that if that's the way it came out.

These excerpts from oral argument illustrate appellate counsel's failure to present his client's case in its most favorable posture. This performance fell far below the range that is professionally acceptable.[133]

Justice Raymond Ehrlich, Florida Supreme Court

_____

Mr. Conner's courtroom comments are stunning, but they pale in comparison to one attorney's "epic fail" during a hearing in Nevada bankruptcy court. Bankruptcy Judge Bruce Markell's vivid depiction of the hapless Mr. Mondejar is one that, if it weren't horrifying, would be hilarious.

The hearing on this Rule 9011 Order to Show Cause did not start auspiciously. After reserving a half-day for the hearing, the court waited to call the matter to allow debtors' counsel, who was subject to the order and whose tardy arrival the court anticipated, extra time to arrive. After waiting almost ten minutes, the court took appearances, and only one lawyer – for a creditor – entered an appearance. One debtor was also present.

Without any appearance by the attorney or law firm named in the Order to Show Cause, the court indicated it would take the matter under submission and then prepared to adjourn. At this point, the debtor present asked to be heard, and the court allowed him to speak. As he was expressing his concerns about the poor quality of his counsel's representation, his attorney – Jeremy Mondejar of the law firm of Barry Levinson & Associates – finally arrived. He was approximately 15 minutes late. As he approached the lectern, he turned on his laptop computer, balanced it in one hand, and began scanning its screen apparently to determine what the hearing was about. He then made his appearance.

The lawyer's subsequent performance, as detailed below, shows that he was unaware of what had been filed in the case and ignorant of the contents of the Order to Show Cause at issue. He floundered, showing an almost complete lack of preparation. It was painful for all in the courtroom, from the client who saw his money being wasted, to the court staff who all too often had seen similar performances from the same attorney, to the court who had to endure silences – sometimes approaching 30 seconds – as Mr. Mondejar attempted to understand and answer the court's questions from information on his computer screen.

Were there ever a time to use "fail," as the contemporary vernacular permits, it is now, and in reference to this deplorable display of legal representation: it was an epic fail.

The events leading up to Mr. Mondejar's flub are not particularly unusual …

The court's September 23, 2011 order not only denied the OST Motion, but it also set an order to show cause given the circumstances under which Mr. Levinson's office submitted it. In particular, it required Mr. Levinson's office to appear and show cause why the filing of the OST Motion did not violate rule 9011. (*Id.* at 1). After the court informed counsel of its concerns, the order specifically advised counsel to be prepared to discuss the following at the hearing on the order to show cause:

i.   [W]hy he filed an OST Motion for the same motion, Dkt. No. 61, which was previously opposed and which this court [previously denied];

ii.   Why he has failed to disclose both the previous motion and the order denying same in his OST Motion; and

iii. Why he did not notify the party who opposed the previous motion in the attorney information sheet as required by Local Rule 9006(a) (and why the date of notification of the Office of the United Sates Trustee was in June, when the OST Motion is dated in September.

(Id. at 1-2). The court also warned counsel that he should be prepared to address "why the OST Motion, which does not contain any information that would help the court find a basis upon which to grant relief requested, does not violate [Rule] 9011." ...

The court scheduled the show cause hearing for October 12, 2011 at 9:30 a.m. (*Id.* at 1). It was the only matter on calendar, and the court had set aside a half day for it. The court, having anticipated that counsel would be late, waited to call the matter almost 10 minutes after its schedule time. (Tr. Of Show Cause Hr'g, Dkt. No. 79, p. 3). With only counsel for Bank of Nevada entering an appearance, the court the matter under submission and prepared to adjourn. (*Id.* at 4). When one of the Debtors, Dr. James Spickelmier, asked to be heard, the court went back on the record. (*Id.*).

Dr. Spickelmier expressed his dissatisfaction with the representation he had received from Mr. Levinson's office. (*Id.*). He stated that counsel had previously failed to appear in court, that counsel had twice assured him that he would appear at the show cause hearing, and that counsel had received payment of over $5,000 for services rendered in this case. (*Id.* at 4-5).

At approximately 9:45 a.m., almost 15 minutes after the hearing's schedule time, Mr. Mondejar, an attorney from Mr. Levinson's office, interrupted Dr. Spickelmier and entered an appearance as set forth in the introduction above. (*Id.* at 6). When asked why he was 15 minutes late, Mr. Mondejar explained that he "just got caught up in traffic, and … was trying to look up some notes … on-line." (*Id.*). From that point, Mr. Mondejar continued to stare at his laptop computer as he struggled to respond to the simplest of queries by the court.

As he read from his laptop, Mr. Mondejar successfully identified the matter before the court: "this is [the] order to show cause for the vacation of … the order to dismiss." (*Id.* at 7). But Mr. Mondejar only managed to tread water for so long; he painfully floundered through the remainder of the hearing.

When the court asked Mr. Mondejar for his response to the Order to Show Cause, eyes fixated on his computer screen, he replied:

> Okay. We are going to convert this. We're going to convert this to a Chapter 11, and he was over the debt limit for a 13. And we believe it's in the best interest, and it's just that we … didn't have the proper time to do all that stuff, and he's over the debt limit, so, I mean, we just need the time to do that stuff, your Honor.

(*Id.* at 7-8).

In an attempt to shepherd Mr. Mondejar through the hearing, the court quoted portions of the Order to Show Cause. Specifically, the court directed Mr. Mondejar's attention to its request for admissible evidence demonstrating the existence of the prejudice referred to in the Levinson Affidavit, the prejudice which supposedly necessitated an order shortening time. (*Id.* at 8-9). The only evidence Mr. Mondejar was prepared to offer, after consulting with Dr. Spickelmier during the hearing, was that a notice of foreclosure had been placed on the Debtors' door two weeks before the hearing. This action, however, would have occurred *after* the filing of the OST Motion. (*Id.* at 11).

Similarly disappointing was Mr. Mondejar's explanation for why Mr. Levinson's office had filed a motion, to be heard on shortened time, that was identical to a previous motion, which the court had denied, and why the later filing contained no mention of the previous denial. (*Id.*). He had none. (*Id.*). All he had was what he could read from his computer screen. (*Id.* at 1). This was the lowest moment in attorney representation the court has ever witnessed. ...

The work counsel performed for the Debtors in this case reflects a lack of competence and diligence that does not deserve to be compensated. Initially, Mr. Levinson's office filed a case for Debtors for which they were not eligible ... [it] then negotiated a stipulation for conversion or dismissal with the Chapter 13 Trustee, but failed to comply with it, resulting in the dismissal of Debtors' case. Counsel then attempted to remedy this failing by moving for reconsideration, but he did not appear at the hearing on the motion. Thereafter, counsel moved for an order shortening time on a motion identical to the one the court previously heard and denied on regular time, without citing to any legal authority that supported the filing. Worse, when the court held the hearing on the Order to Show Cause issued with respect to these filings, counsel failed to provide any support for its actions, despite being warned to come to court prepared to provide such support. Given the poor quality of the services rendered by Mr. Levinson's office in this matter, the court finds that the reasonable value of those services is zero, that is, $0.00...[134]

Judge Bruce A. Markell, Bankruptcy Court,
District of Nevada

_____

The outcome of this "epic" smack down? A public reprimand, $5,000 in disgorged legal fees, special affidavits and disclosures to clients and the court for the next three years, and a referral to the state Bar of Nevada to investigate whether further disciplinary proceedings are warranted.[135] In fairness to Mr. Mondejar, it appears he began working for Levinson & Associates only a few weeks before being saddled with the hearing. Mr. Levinson's signature appeared on the pleadings in the case and his firm was held jointly responsible for all sanctions.

The performances of Mssrs. Mondejar, Conner, Greco and Rakofsky makes one wonder how they managed to successfully navigate law school and the rigors of their state's Bar exam. Perhaps their clients would have been better served by proceeding *pro se*?

It's not likely. Whatever the follies and foibles of the attorneys described above, they are nothing compared to the antics of many *pro se* litigants.

CHAPTER 8: No Pity for *Pro Se*

As a general rule, and to the chagrin of licensed attorneys everywhere, most judges are exceedingly patient with *pro se* litigants. Judges are sensitive to the high cost of litigation and will bend over backwards to accommodate self-represented parties who attempt to comply with court rules and present their case. That being said, judges have virtually no patience for *pro se* litigants who use the legal system for their own personal amusement.

Case in chief is Above the Law's recurring *"Pro Se* Litigant of the Day" and federal prison's most prolific litigator, Jonathan Lee Riches© (for those unfamiliar with Mr. Riches, he claims his name is copyrighted).[136] Mr. Riches has filed over one thousand lawsuits since 2006 and has sued a litany of individuals and corporations, including (but certainly not limited to) Bill Belichick, George W. Bush, Martha Stewart, Jared Loughner, Britney Spears, Jeff Gordon, Steve Jobs, Michael Vick, Perez Hilton, Pervez Musharraf, Benazir Bhutto, Somali Pirates, the

Immigration and Naturalization Service, Rockstar Games, the Guinness Book of World Records, the "13 Tribes of Israel," the Holy Grail, The Garden of Eden, the Roman Empire, the Eiffel Tower, Nordic Gods, the planetoid Pluto and the book *Mein Kamph.*[137] Although Mr. Riches' lawsuits provide nearly endless source material for the legal blogosphere, federal district court judges have not been similarly amused.

On March 27, 2008, District Court Judge Willis B. Hunt noted that Mr. Riches' 271 lawsuits pending in Georgia's Southern District were "substantially and deleteriously straining the Court's limited resources," and that "something must be done now to curtail this completely unnecessary burden."[138] The court ordered Mr. Riches permanently enjoined from filing or attempting to file any new lawsuit without prior leave of the court. Of course, Mr. Riches was not filing claims solely in the Southern District of Georgia. Even as Judge Hunt was slapping down Mr. Riches' multitude of lawsuits, Judge Frederick P. Stamp in the Northern District of West Virginia was dismissing another 48 lawsuits filed by Mr. Riches on the grounds that "they [were] irrational and wholly incredible."[139] Neither opinion deterred Mr. Riches, who today holds a record for the most lawsuits filed by a *pro se* litigant and is notorious within the legal community.

The Jonathan Lee Riches© example illustrates how judges' frustration with frivolous lawsuits is fully justified. How is a judge expected to respond to a lawsuit against the Nordic gods? And so, while there's no glory in taking pot-shots at *pro se* litigants, and while stern words are unlikely to stem the tide of frivolous lawsuits, sometimes judges simply can't help themselves.

Although judges are often hesitant to benchslap *pro se* plaintiffs, they appear more likely to do so when a lawsuit gets personal. For example, in *Washington v. Alaimo*, *pro se* plaintiff Matthew Washington named a number of district court judges in his complaint and proceeded to file a series of frivolous motions. He ultimately filed more than 75 motions, including the infamous "Motion to Kiss My Ass," in which he moved "all Americans at large and one corrupt Judge Smith [to] kiss my got [sic] damn ass sorry mother fucker you.'" The resulting docket is among the most amusing in the federal court system. From the U.S. Justice Department's "PACER" website:

10/26/1995	17	MOTION by Matthew Washington to kiss my ass with brief in support.
04/05/1996	27	ORDER mooting [17-1] motion to kiss my ass.
04/18/1996	29	ORDER denying pltf's "Motion to Kiss My Ass" because it does not present a question for adjudication

Following Mr. Washington's hand-written "Motion to Kiss My Ass," Judge William Moore ordered him to respond to a motion for Rule 11 sanctions. When Mr. Washington did not respond as ordered, Judge Moore dismissed the lawsuit and concluded his opinion with the following benchslap summarizing Mr. Washington's legal antics:

…This Court also observes that this is not the first instance in which Plaintiff has abused the civil right forum of this Court provided through 42 U.S.C. § 1983 and finds that certain restrictions, as outlined below, need to be placed upon prospective lawsuits initiated by Plaintiff in order to protect parties from abusive litigation and to protect the federal judiciary's integrity of purpose. …

Since his commitment to the state prison system, Plaintiff has become a frequent litigant within the federal courts seeking relief through the auspices of 42 U.S.C. § 1983. The Clerk of Court for the Superior Court of Chatham County has also informed this Court that Plaintiff is frequently suing for various forms of relief through the state court system as well. What distinguishes Plaintiff from most prisoner litigants in federal courts is that he pays his filing fee rather than submit an application to proceed *in forma pauperis* under the provisions of 28 U.S.C. § 1915. It has come to the attention of this Court that Plaintiff's litigation practice is largely, if not entirely, underwritten by the Federal Treasury as he periodically receives a substantial check for veterans' disability benefits. By paying his filing fee, Plaintiff has thus far avoided the filter of the 28 U.S.C. § 1915(d) frivolity review. As a result, patently frivolous lawsuits have languished in this district longer than would otherwise be warranted with other prisoner litigants.

Plaintiff has shown in his dealings with the courts in this District that he lacks the ability or will to govern his suits with the civility and order required by the Local Rules and by the Federal Rules of Civil Procedure. He has wasted the time of many an innocent party and he has flippantly used the resources of the judiciary with his abusive motions filing practice.

In *Matthew Washington v. Bobby Whitworth, et al.*, 6:91cv87, this Court's experience with Plaintiff began. In that case, Plaintiff filed the Complaint on November 8, 1991, and soon commenced his motion filings practice. In February 1992, he moved to change venue. Then, he initiated the trademark of his practice: the Motion to Amend Complaint. He moved to amend his complaint on March 6, 1992, on April 15, 1992, and on December 14, 1992. After a couple allowances of amendment, Judge Dudley H. Bowen, Jr., began denying Plaintiff's motions to amend. Soon thereafter he moved to disqualify Judge Bowen and began filing "Extraordinary Motions to Amend" including one which desired to add the United States Secret Service as a party.

> "Then, he initiated the trademark of his practice: the Motion to Amend Complaint."

Plaintiff began filing frivolous motions on a weekly basis and, in that relatively simple civil rights lawsuit, he ended up filing more than seventy-five pleadings, all of which required the considered attention of this Court and Judge Bowen. These motions included "Motion to Behoove an Inquisition" and "Motion for *Judex Delegatus*" and "Motion for Restoration of Sanity" and "Motion for Deinstitutionalization." In one instance, he indicated the recreational tilt of his litigation when he filed a "Motion for Publicity" regarding a trial which had been set for March 23, 1995, in Statesboro. At the time of trial, Plaintiff filed a "Motion to Vacate Jurisdiction"

> "These motions included 'Motion to Behoove an Inquisition' and... 'Motion for Restoration of Sanity' and 'Motion for Deinstitutionalization.'"

which was denied. Even after judgment as a matter of law was entered against him at the trial, Plaintiff did not perceive his case as complete. He renewed the filing of "Extraordinary Motions to Amend" and filed his appeals, fees paid, with the United States Court of Appeals for the Eleventh Circuit.

After one year of motions filing after the case had been closed, this Court ordered Plaintiff to quit submitting motions in a closed case and directed the Clerk to return to Plaintiff any further pleading filed by him. Plaintiff "oneupped" the Clerk when he filed a Notice of Appeal from that order; the notice, of course, had to be placed in the case file.

In *Matthew Washington v. James T. Morris, et al.* 4:93cv114, Plaintiff set out to sue a host of individuals, including the Superior Court judge who presided over his the Hodgson murder trial and the attorney who defended him in that trial. Plaintiff filed the complaint on May 20, 1993, and sought to amend it on June 7, 1993, July 21, 1993, July 23, 1993, November 2, 1993, November 5, 1993, December 14, 1993, December 22, 1993, January 23, 1995, March 2, 1995, March 29, 1995, and on October 20, 1995. At least one of these Motions to Amend sought to add Magistrate Judge James E. Graham as a party defendant. Plaintiff filed fifty-four pleadings in that case, all of which required the considered attention of Judge Anthony A. Alaimo or magistrate Graham. The motions ranged from the mundane, such as "Motion for Change of Venue," to the arcane, such as "Motion for *Cesset pro Cessus*" and "Motion for *Judex Delegatus*," to the curious, such as "Motion for *Nunc pro Tunc*" and "Motion for Psychoanalysis," to the outlandish, such as "Motion to Impeach Judge Alaimo" and "Motion to Renounce Citizenship" and "Motion to Exhume Body of Alex

Hodgson." Plaintiff also filed numerous interlocutory appeals, which required the attention and utilization of the resources of the Court of Appeals. The case was disposed of on the pleadings in Defendants' favor. Plaintiff has filed an appeal.

Plaintiff's other cases in this district demonstrate that his litigation practice continues with the same themes as described above. In *Matthew Washington v. Dr. Joseph H. Owens, Jr.*, 6:94cv39, Plaintiff filed some ten motions to amend, moved to disqualify the undersigned judge, and also expressed his contempt for the undersigned judge by filing a "Motion to Invoke and Execute Rule 15--Retroactive Note: The Court's School Days are Over". This Court dismissed Plaintiff's complaint upon motion by the Defendant. The case currently is on appeal. In *Matthew Washington v. Ronald Fountain, et al.*, 6:94cv120, Plaintiff has already filed thirteen motions to amend, including one which sought to add President Clinton as a party. Plaintiff also sought to disqualify the undersigned judge and again invoked the mysterious "Rule 15." The case has been reassigned to Chief Judge B. Avant Edenfield and is still pending.

In the instant case, Plaintiff has sued all of the judges and one magistrate judge from this District as well as one judge and one magistrate judge from the Middle District of Georgia. Plaintiff also unsuccessfully tried to join Judge Michael Karpf of the Superior Court of Chatham County and United States Senator Sam Nunn. His five motions to amend are overshadowed by the "Motion to Kiss My Ass" which Plaintiff filed (apparently to express his frustration with Magistrate Judge G.R. Smith's refusal to allow

> "His five motions to amend are overshadowed by the 'Motion to Kiss My Ass.'"

the addition of Judge Karpf and Senator Nunn). This case has been pending less than one year and already Plaintiff has filed three interlocutory appeals. Likewise, in *Matthew Washington v. R.D. Collins, et al.*, 6:95cv113, Plaintiff has already filed three frivolous interlocutory appeals in a case which is only several months old. [Footnote 1 omitted]

In *Matthew Washington v. Dr. Joseph H. Owens*, 6:95cv214, Plaintiff has filed a "Motion for Skin Change Operation" in which he desired the government to fund a sex change for him. When Magistrate Judge W. Leon Barfield denied the motion, Plaintiff filed a "Motion to Impeach" the magistrate. He also unsuccessfully sought to add the undersigned judge as a party defendant.

In another case which had been originally filed in the Northern District of Georgia, 6:96cv54, Plaintiff sued the same judges as in this case and also added Ted Turner of CNN International for good measure: "Mr. Turner, a fellow Georgian, is and has violated the 'Free Press' of which he 'supposedly stands' with his cartel and CBS endeavors to do the same." Recently, he filed a "Motion for Catered Food Services" in which he complained about the prison food and moved for a court order allowing him to "receive catered food from some credible responsible business establishment preferred and paid for by Plaintiff."

"Recently, he filed a 'Motion for Catered Food Services.'"

These are just some examples from some of Plaintiff's recent litigation adventures. Prior to this decade, Plaintiff had a long history of litigation within this District. His recreational litigation has gone on for entirely too long and at great expense to the American taxpayer. Too many resources have been wasted and too many innocent people harassed. This Court now considers what discretion it has to prevent the future waste of judicial resources...

This Court finds that Plaintiff has abused the judiciary and that his abuse has lingered longer than would otherwise be tolerated from normal prisoner plaintiffs because of Plaintiff's status as a pay-to-play litigant. The time has come to take the rattle from the baby and impose some form and discipline upon Plaintiff's law practice within this and other federal courts.

Accordingly, this Court hereby **ENJOINS** Plaintiff from filing a lawsuit in this or any other federal district court unless the following conditions are met:

1. In addition to paying the $120.00 filing fee which Plaintiff has already demonstrated the ability to pay, Plaintiff must post a $1,500.00 contempt bond with the Clerk of Court. [Footnote 2 omitted] This bond will be held by the Clerk of Court and, if Plaintiff has conducted the affairs in his case appropriately within the realm of Federal Rule of Civil Procedure 11, the bond will be returned to Plaintiff at the conclusion of his case. (Footnote 3: This provision is created to ensure that Plaintiff will not act as he has in the instant case in which he harshly abused several members of the Court and the American taxpayers (who have completely funded his litigious exploits) and then fail to respond to a Rule 11 show-cause order.)

2. A signed affidavit shall accompany his complaint in which Plaintiff swears that he has read Federal Rule of Civil Procedure 11 and that he will abide by the tenets listed therein. . .

This Court is quite sure that, if the villagers who heard the boy cry 'wolf' one time too many had some form of reassurance that the boy's last cry was sincere, they would have responded appropriately and he would be alive instead of being dinner for the ravenous canine. If anything, that story teaches that repetitious tomfoolery can result in disaster for the knave. This Court will not turn a deaf ear to Plaintiff's future cries. However, it will require Plaintiff to structure his pleas for help in a more sincere manner so that the energies of the villagers are not wasted on the repeated runs up the grassy hill atop which the mischievous boy sits laughing.[140]

Judge William Moore, USDC,
Southern District of Georgia

———————————————

There's an interesting postscript to the *Washington* case. Plaintiff's appeal to the Eleventh Circuit was dismissed in April 2003, but in January 2010 he moved for reconsideration. Accompanying his "Motion for Reconsideration" was the following hand-written "Motion to Apologize":

Come now Holy Rev. Matthew Washington and apologize to this court and all defendants in the above captioned case and

I apologize to the American people for filing that motion to kiss my ass.[141]

Sadly, the Bench was not in a forgiving mood. Mr. Washington's "Motion to Apologize" was denied in a cursory opinion by Chief Judge Lisa G. Wood on March 29, 2011.[142]

District courts bear the heaviest burden of frivolous lawsuits filed by *pro se* plaintiffs and, as a result, are more prone to benchslapping than their appellate peers. In the *Washington* case, the District Court entertained nearly 75 frivolous motions before laying the smack down. But even appellate courts can lose patience with *pro se* litigants when pushed to extremes.

For example, in *Schlessinger v. Salimes*, plaintiff David Schlessinger sued for being forced to leave a restaurant after he delivered a lengthy, angry and disruptive tirade about the doneness of his steak. In an opinion that labels plaintiff and his claims as "nutty," "goofy," "frivolous," "malicious," "absurd," "doomed," "weak" and "incoherent," Chief Judge Frank Easterbrook of the Seventh Circuit delivered a blistering benchslap:

> David Schlessinger and two friends visited Anthony's Steakhouse in Geneva, Wisconsin, for dinner on January 8, 1994. Schlessinger ordered his steak medium-well done. Before the main course arrived, Schlessinger deemed that he was "receiving substandard service at the restaurant, so I demanded better service." Judging the meat he received "burned," Schlessinger complained long and loud. George Condos, the owner, told him that the food had been properly prepared and asked him to stop disturbing the other patrons. Schlessinger was unwilling to eat the food, to leave, or to pay until his demand

198

for a new entree had been met. Schlessinger's affidavit continues: "I feared trouble by the escalating situation and called the police [from my cellular phone] to get the situation corrected." George Salimes and another officer answered the call. Condos suggested to the officers that Schlessinger might be under the influence of drugs. Salimes told Schlessinger that, unless he paid the tab and left, he would be arrested for disorderly conduct and theft of services. The trio then paid and left.

Most people dissatisfied with a restaurant's service or cuisine would tell their friends not to go, resolve not to return themselves, and perhaps write a letter to the editor of the local newspaper or the Better Business Bureau, then let the matter drop. But having played the wise guy in calling the police, Schlessinger encored that performance by filing this suit against Condos, Salimes, and everyone else in or out of sight-including the Town of Geneva, the Town Board and its members, the Town's police department, and the Town's chief of police. According to the complaint, most of the defendants are liable under 42 U.S.C. § 1983 for an unconstitutional seizure of his person-even though he walked out of the restaurant unhindered. Condos and the Restaurant were sued under the diversity jurisdiction on a variety of state-law theories. None of the claims reached first base. The district court dismissed those against Condos and the Restaurant after finding that Schlessinger could not obtain damages exceeding the jurisdictional minimum (then $50,000). The court granted summary judgment to Salimes on the ground of qualified immunity. Claims against the remaining defendants collapsed because Schlessinger neglected to inform the court how they could be liable. He asserted that they were indifferent to his rights, but that is not enough for liability. After judgment, Schlessinger attempted to rectify the deficiency by a motion under Fed.R.Civ.P. 60(b)(6), which the district judge denied out of hand. Schlessinger has filed appeals from both the judgment and the order denying the Rule 60(b) motion.

This goofy lawsuit deservedly met an abrupt end in the district court. Frivolous at the outset, and likely maliciously retaliatory as well, the case has deteriorated on appeal. Consider for example the question whether the complaint satisfies the jurisdictional minimum amount in controversy. Plaintiffs receive the benefit of all doubt: a court may not dismiss the claim unless it "appear[s] to a legal certainty that the claim is really for less than the jurisdictional amount". St. Paul Mercury Indemnity Co. v. Red Cab Co., 303 U.S. 283, 289, 58 S.Ct. 586, 590, 82 L.Ed. 845 (1938). Yet a plaintiff challenged to show that the recovery could exceed the requisite level cannot just appeal to the judge's druthers; he must show how the rules of law, applied to the facts of his case, could produce such an award. *Wellness Community [registered]-National v. Wellness House*, 70 F.3d 46, 49-50 (Seventh Cir.1995). Schlessinger was not arrested, and the check for all three diners was only $100 (some of which doubtless represents drinks and appetizers, and therefore is not in controversy). He himself called the police, initiating the events of which he complains. He accuses Condos of slander for telling Salimes that Schlessinger might be high on drugs. We suppose that this statement is defamatory and shall assume not only that the complaint adequately alleges malice but also that Wisconsin authorizes punitive damages for statements to the police-although it has a strong privilege (which Schlessinger does not discuss) for allegations of crime made to police for the purpose of initiating a bona fide investigation. *Otten v. Schutt*, 15 Wis.2d 497, 113 N.W.2d 152 (1962); *Joseph v. Baars*, 142 Wis. 390, 125

N.W. 913(1910). Does Wisconsin authorize punitive awards as high as $50,000 in the absence of any concrete injury? Schlessinger did not cite in the district court a single case addressing that subject, or any other theory of damages.

On appeal, his indifference to Wisconsin's law persists. . . . Because he took his cue from the newspapers rather than from the law books, Schlessinger's lawyer (yes, he has one) neglected to notice that many jury awards are trimmed as legally unjustified. Runaway juries occasionally return mammoth verdicts; this interesting social phenomenon does not effectively abolish the jurisdictional minimum in diversity litigation, as Schlessinger seems to believe...

> "On appeal, his indifference to Wisconsin's law persists..."

Once again, things have gone downhill on appeal. Instead of addressing the reasons he lost, Schlessinger argues that a district court's order denying a motion under Rule 60(b)(6) should be reviewed *de novo* by the court of appeals. The contention is nutty. . . At all events, the contention is beside the point: by omitting any argument that the district court's decision in favor of these defendants was mistaken, Schlessinger has rendered the standard of review irrelevant. . .

Quite aside from the fact that Schlessinger's brief does not offer a coherent (indeed, any) argument for abandoning *Rakovich v. Wade*, 850 F.2d 1180, 1201-02 (Seventh Cir.1988) (*en banc*), there is the fact that judges have been told by the Supreme Court that, because immunity protects public officials from the burden of litigation, courts must resolve immunity defenses before trial, and when possible before discovery. *See Hunter v.*

Bryant, 502 U.S. 224, 227, 112 S.Ct. 534, 536, 116 L.Ed.2d 589 (1991); *Harlow v. Fitzgerald*, 457 U.S. 800, 818, 102 S.Ct. 2727, 2738, 73 L.Ed.2d 396 (1982). Schlessinger does not deign to discuss the decisions of the Supreme Court that undergird the cases he asks us to overrule.

Schlessinger's suit is absurd and likely malicious. It trivializes the constitutional rights he asks us to vindicate. If your meal is not tasty, you do not throw a tantrum, upset the other diners, and then sue the mayor of the town where the restaurant is located. Perhaps the dispute about the bill was meet for small-claims court in Wisconsin; it was nothing to make a federal case about. The appeal is even weaker than the original complaint. Suits and appeals such as this not only bring the courts into disrepute but also divert scarce judicial time from other litigants who have serious claims or defenses. We therefore direct Schlessinger and his attorney to show cause, within 14 days, why they should not be penalized under Fed. R.App. P. 38 and Circuit Rule 38 for pursuing a frivolous appeal.[143]

> "Schlessinger's suit is absurd and likely malicious. It trivializes the constitutional rights he asks us to vindicate. If your meal is not tasty, you do not throw a tantrum ... and then sue the mayor."

Chief Judge Frank Easterbook, Seventh Circuit

Careful readers likely noted that Mr. Schlessinger was not, in fact, a *pro se* plaintiff. Judge Easterbrook himself appeared surprised at this: "Because he took his cue from the newspapers rather than from the law books, Schlessinger's lawyer (yes, he has one) neglected to notice that many jury awards are trimmed as legally unjustified." Judge Easterbrook makes almost no distinction between plaintiff and counsel, which is itself a staggering benchslap.

As a reminder that recovery from a judicial takedown is possible, it's worth following the subsequent career of Mr. Schlessinger's attorney, Andrew J. Shaw. Mr. Shaw was born in South Korea and raised in Minnesota, and was just four years out of Marquette Law School when he argued the *Schlessinger* appeal before the Seventh Circuit in 1996. He remains an active member in good standing of the Wisconsin bar.

In 1999, just seven years out of law school, he adopted an "if you can't beat 'em join 'em" mentality and ran for judge in Milwaukee County. He received 26-percent of the vote, even while coping with home foreclosure and bankruptcy relating, perhaps unsurprisingly, to cases he was involved with as an attorney. In 2008, Mr. Shaw became the first Asian-American candidate for Mayor of Milwaukee and garnered more than 20% of the vote while running against Democratic incumbent and former gubernatorial candidate Tom Barrett. He continues to practice law and remains actively involved in his community.[144]

Although most *pro se* judicial smack downs involve legal actions initiated by plaintiffs, *pro se* parties can also bring down the thunder when on the defensive. In *Trustees of Columbia University v. Jacobsen*, a former university student was sued by his alma mater for non-payment of student loans. Rather than repay the loans, the student filed a counterclaim against the university for fraud based on false representations. His claim alleged that, contrary to university promotional literature, the school failed to teach him wisdom, truth, justice, beauty, spirituality and other essential skills. The following benchslap resulted.

The attempt of the counterclaim, inartistically drawn as it is, as to state a cause of action in deceit. The necessary elements of that action are by now hornbook law: a false representation, knowledge or belief on the part of the person making the representation that it is false, an intention that the other party act thereon, reasonable reliance by such party in so doing, and resultant damage to him. *See Prosser on Torts* (2d ed.1955), s 86, p. 523; *Louis Schlesinger Co. v. Wilson*, 22 N.J. 576, 585-586, 127 A.2d 13 (1956).

We are in complete agreement with the trial court that the counterclaim fails to establish the very first element, false representation, basic to any action in deceit. Plaintiff stands by very quotation relied on by defendant. Only by reading into them the imagined meanings he attributes to them can one conclude – and the conclusion would be a most tenuous, insubstantial one – that Columbia University represented it could teach wisdom, truth, justice, beauty, spirituality and all the other qualities set out in the 50 counts of the counterclaim.

A sampling from the quotations cited by defendant will suffice as illustration. Defendant quotes from a Columbia College brochure stating that Columbia College provides a liberal arts education. A liberal arts course has extremely positive values of its own. Chief among these, perhaps, is something which has been a principal aim of Columbia College from the beginning: It develops the whole man. (Columbia's) aim remains constant: to foster in its students a desire to learn, a habit of critical judgment, and a deep-rooted sense of personal and social responsibility. (I)ts liberal arts course pursues this aim in five ways. (1) It brings you into firsthand contact with the major intellectual ideas that have helped to shape human thinking and the course of human events. (2) It gives you a broader acquaintance with the rest of the world. (3) It guides you toward an understanding of people and their motivations. (4) It leads you to a comprehending knowledge of the scientific world. (5) It helps you acquire facility in the art of communication.'

He then cites the motto of Columbia College and Columbia University: *'In lumine tuo videbimus lumen'* ('In your light we shall see light'), and the inscription over the college chapel: 'Wisdom dwelleth in the heart of him that hath understanding.' He also refers to an address of the president of Columbia University at its bicentennial convocation:

'There can never have been a time in the history of the world when men had greater need of wisdom. I mean an understanding of man's relationship to his fellow men and to the universe. To this task of educational leadership in a troubled time and in an uncertain world, Columbia, like other great centers of learning in free societies, unhesitatingly dedicates itself.'

We have thoroughly combed all the statements upon which defendant relies in his counterclaim, as well as the exhibits he handed up to the trial judge, including one of 59 pages setting out his account of the circumstances leading to the present action. They add up to nothing more than a fairly complete exposition of Columbia's objectives, desires and hopes, together with factual statements as to the nature of some of the courses included in its curricula. As plaintiff correctly observes, what defendant is seeking to do is to assign to the quoted excerpts a construction and interpretation peculiarly subjective to him and completely unwarranted by the plain sense and meaning of the language used. To defendant a college is not 'Mark Hopkins at one end of a log and the student at the other,' but his dream of a universal scholar *cum* philosopher *cum* humanitarian at one end of the school bench and defendant at the other.

At the heart of defendant's counterclaim is a single complaint. He concedes that:

'I have really only one charge against Columbia: that it does not teach Wisdom as it claims to do. From this charge ensues an endless number of charges, of which I have selected fifty at random. I am prepared to show that each of these fifty claims in turn is false, though the central issue is that of Columbia's pretense of teaching Wisdom.'

We agree with the trial judge that wisdom is not a subject which can be taught and that no rational person would accept such a claim made by any man or institution. We find nothing in the record to establish that Columbia represented, expressly or even by way of impression, that it could or would teach wisdom or the several qualities which defendant insists are 'synonyms for or aspects of the same Quality.' The matter is perhaps best summed up in the

> "We agree with the trial judge that wisdom is not a subject which can be taught..."

supporting affidavit of the Dean of Columbia College, where he said that 'All that any college can do through its teachers, libraries, laboratories and other facilities is to endeavor to teach the student the known facts, acquaint him with the nature of those matters which are unknown, and thereby assist him in developing mentally, morally and physically. Wisdom is a hoped-for end product of education, experience and ability which many seek and many fail to attain.'

Defendant's extended argument lacks the element of fraudulent representation indispensable to any action of deceit. We note, in passing, that he has cited no legal authority whatsoever for his position. Instead, he has submitted a dictionary definition of 'wisdom' and quotations from such works as the Bhagavad-Gita, the Mundaka Upanishad, the Analects of Confucius and the Koran; excerpts from Euripides, Plato and Menander; and references to the Bible. Interesting though these may be, they do not support defendant's indictment of Columbia. If his pleadings, affidavit and exhibits demonstrate anything, it is indeed the validity of what Pope said in his Moral Essays:

> '*A little learning is a dangerous thing;*
> *Drink deep, or taste not the Pierian spring*'

The papers make clear that through the years defendant's interest has shifted from civil engineering to social work, then to physics, and finally to English and creative writing. In college he became increasingly critical of his professors and his courses; in his last year he attended classes only when he chose and rejected the regimen of examinations and term papers. When his non-attendance at classes and his poor work in the senior year were called to his attention by the Columbia Dean of Students, he replied in a lengthy letter that 'I want to learn, but I must do it my own way. I realize my behavior is non-conforming, but in these times when there are so many forces that demand conformity I hope I will find Columbia willing to grant some freedom to a student who wants to be a literary artist.' In short, he chose to judge Columbia's educational system by the shifting standards of his own fancy, and now seeks to place his failure at Columbia's door on the theory that it had deliberately misrepresented that it taught wisdom.[145]

> "He chose to judge Columbia's educational system by the shifting standards of his own fancy, and now seeks to place his failure at Columbia's door..."

Judge Sidney Goldmann, New Jersey Superior Court,
Appellate Division

———————————

As the *Washington*, *Schlessinger* and *Jacobsen* opinions demonstrate, there is no shortage of frivolous lawsuits warranting judicial smack downs. But benchslapping a *pro se* litigant for filing a frivolous claim is like punishing a baby for crying; they just don't know any better. Punishment is more deserved when licensed attorneys engage in misconduct, and the greatest benchslaps of all are reserved for those attorneys who turn the time-honored process on its head and publicly insult the bench.

CHAPTER 9: Reverse Benchslaps

There's no doubt litigation can get heated. But it is a special breed of professional litigator who throws caution to the wind to express her anger to the very judge deciding her case. When such litigators get benchslapped, they slap the bench right back. This is a risky legal maneuver David Lat refers to as the "reverse benchslap."

David "Mac" McKeand, a solo practitioner working out of Houston, had the good (or bad) fortune to appear before renowned Seventh Circuit jurist and benchslapper Richard Posner. When Mr. McKeand failed to address potentially dispositive adverse authority in his brief, Judge Posner set aside several pages to address Mr. KcKeand's perceived deficiency:

> When there is apparently dispositive precedent, an appellant may urge its overruling or distinguishing or reserve a challenge to it for a petition for certiorari but may not simply ignore it. We don't know the thinking that led the appellants' counsel in these two cases to do that. But we do know that the

two sets of cases out of which the appeals arise, involving the blood-products and Bridgestone/Firestone tire litigations, generated many transfers under the doctrine of forum non conveniens, three of which we affirmed in the two ignored precedents. There are likely to be additional such appeals; maybe appellants think that if they ignore our precedents their appeals will not be assigned to the same panel as decided the cases that established the precedents. Whatever the reason, such advocacy is unacceptable.

The ostrich is a noble animal, but not a proper model for an appellate advocate. (Not that ostriches really bury their heads in the sand when threatened; don't be fooled by the picture below.) The "ostrich-like tactic of pretending that potentially dispositive authority against a litigant's contention does not exist is as unprofessional as it is pointless." *Mannheim Video, Inc. v. County of Cook*, 884 F.2d 1043, 1047 (Seventh Cir. 1989), quoting *Hill v. Norfolk & Western Ry.*, 814 F.2d 1192, 1198 (Seventh Cir. 1987).

The attorney in the vehicular accident case, David S. "Mac" McKeand, is especially culpable, because he filed his opening brief as well as his reply brief after the Abad decision yet mentioned it in neither brief despite the heavy reliance that opposing counsel placed on it in their response brief. In contrast, counsel in the bloodproducts appeal could not have referred to either Abad or Chang in their opening brief, did try to distinguish Abad (if unpersuasively) in their reply brief, and may have thought that Chang added nothing to Abad. Their advocacy left much to be desired, but McKeand's left more.[146]

AFFIRMED.

Judge Richard Posner, Seventh Circuit

_____

To better illustrate his point, Judge Posner included the photographs above in full color in the official opinion.

But Mr. McKeand didn't take his benchslap lying down. When asked about the benchslap by Joe Pallazzolo of the Wall Street Journal's legal blog, Mr. McKeand retorted that Judge Posner's opinion was "beneath his high level of jurisprudence."[147] He added, "Not only [was the adverse authority] on a different continent, the record we presented had no fewer than ten cases dismissed by Mexican courts proving that Mexico does not have any jurisdiction over foreign defendants." Mr. McKeand concluded with this zinger: "*Abad* was not controlling or even relevant to this case ... In light of all the facts, I can only wonder who really is the ostrich."

Mr. McKeand may have been less upset if he'd known that Judge Posner has a history of inserting ostrich comments into his opinions. Shortly after Judge Posner's opinion was issued, the New York legal blog Simple Justice noted this aside in a 2008 Posner opinion in *United States v. Black*:

> There are three more issues need to be discussed. The first is whether an "ostrich" instruction should have been given. The reference of course is to the legend that ostriches when frightened bury their head in the sand. It is pure legend and a canard on a very distinguished bird. Zoological Society of San Diego, Birds: Ostrich, www.sandiegozoo.org/animalbytes/t-ostrich.html (visited June 12, 2008) ("When an ostrich senses danger and cannot run away, it flops to the ground and remains still, with its head and neck flat on the ground in front of it. Because the head and neck are lightly colored, they blend in with the color of the soil. From a distance, it just looks like the ostrich has buried its head in the sand, because only the body is visible"). It is too late, however, to correct this injustice...[148]

All things considered, Judge Posner may have let Mr. McKreand off easy. And while he may steer clear of the Seventh Circuit for the foreseeable future, Mr. McKreand's comments were far from fighting words.

By contrast, when William P. Smith, a partner at law firm McDermott Will & Emery and the head of its bankruptcy department, told Bankruptcy Judge Laurel M. Isicoff she was "a few French fries short of a Happy Meal," he was served with a blistering order to show cause why he should be permitted to continue practicing in her courtroom.[149] The matter was not resolved until the head of the 1,000 attorney law firm flew to Miami to apologize in person to Judge Isicoff. And when Legal Aid lawyer Arnold Levine made allegedly rude comments to Judge Donna G. Recant of Manhattan Criminal Court, he was ordered to apologize. When Judge Recant determined his apology was inadequate, he was handcuffed and sentenced to ten days in jail.[150] In 1996, Judge Recant also sentenced a man to seven months in jail for cursing her seven times; one month per curse.[151]

The history of harsh discipline described above didn't bode well for Idaho lawyer Eric J. Scott, who in 2011 sought to withdraw from a criminal case based on the extraordinary allegation in his written brief that presiding Judge Thomas Watkins was "lazy; incompetent; biased; prejudiced; or all or some of the above." Mr. Scott then added:

> With all due respect, Counsel simply cannot escape this belief. There is no explanation for this Court's "finding" of a "fact" *that did not exist*. It would be understandable if this Court *overlooked* a fact, this Court *made up a fact*. It just so happens that

this Court made up facts to the advantage of his former employer, the Boise City Prosecutor's Office. Therefore, the Court is either biased toward them, prejudiced against Counsel, too lazy to actually listen to the recording of the relevant interview, or too incompetent to reach the correct conclusion from the facts. Therefore, Counsel lacks faith in this Court's ability to objectively and competently serve as a fact-finder in this case.

For the reasons set forth above, Counsel also has no faith in this Court's ability to competently and objectively interpret the law in this case. The Court's stunningly nonsensical statement of the "test" for determining custody speaks for itself. The Court also did not even understand the rather simple ordinance, and then ironically called into question Counsel's legal abilities. This Court was not impressed with Counsel's legal skills, but suffice it to say that Counsel shares a similar opinion of this Court's abilities to interpret the law and find facts.

Due to Counsel's inability to maintain the requisite level of respect for this Court, Counsel feels that it would be in his client's best interests to withdraw from this matter. Defendant already has the assistance of Co-counsel, who is an outstanding criminal defense attorney, and therefore Defendant will not be prejudiced by Counsel's withdrawal.[152]

Lawyers reading this motion can't help but cower before the impending benchslap. Attorney Mauricio Hernandez of legal blog The Irreverent Lawyer framed the issue this way:

…[G]iven the ethical rules, the potential prejudice to clients and the generalized fear lawyers have about saying unkind things about judges, it's exceedingly rare for a lawyer to attempt to smack down a judge. It's so absurdly unheard of that I'm reminded of what Samuel Johnson mysogynistically said in another albeit nastier context, when you finally hear about such conduct, it's like a 'dog walking on his hind legs. It is not done well; but you are surprised to find it done at all.' This is why news about what Idaho criminal defense lawyer Eric J. Scott did last month in filing his angry "Motion to Withdraw" is so cringe-worthy…"[153]

When Mr. Scott's benchslap finally came, it came in the form of three days and two nights in an Ada County jail. At the time of this printing, his contempt charge is still on appeal.

But on the bright side, Mr. Scott's client was acquitted two weeks after he filed the motion to withdraw, and the open container charge – the subject of the Court's "made up fact" – was dismissed for the reasons set forth in his infamous motion. Despite Mr. Scott's stint in Ada County Jail and the disciplinary charges against him, his client left the courtroom with a clear record and a clean conscience. Mr. Scott's motion may be an exceedingly rare example of the successfully executed "reverse benchslap."

And Mr. Scott had just the right balance of skill and inexperience to pull it off. A law school standout, Mr. Scott later served as a Judicial Law Clerk for Justice W. Jones of the Idaho Supreme Court. In that capacity, he reviewed hundreds of Supreme Court and appellate briefs. Before entering private practice he was a Chief Deputy Prosecutor for Boise County, where he prosecuted individuals accused of a wide variety of crimes. On the other hand, Mr. Scott had been practicing only four years at the time of his (in)famous motion to withdraw, perhaps too junior to know that a standoff between attorney and judge is inherently imbalanced.

What pushed Mr. Scott over the edge? Judge Watkins had insulted Mr. Scott in a memorandum decision, disregarded his legal opinion and denied his motion *in limine* based on "facts" not in the record. With only a handful of weeks before trial and no means of immediately appealing the Court's earlier rulings, Mr. Scott felt he had nothing to lose by lashing out. Of course, any long-term concerns may have been offset by the fact that his client, Mr. Lorimor, was also his brother-in-law. Readers may be pleased to know that Mr. Scott was vindicated when Judge Watkins, in open court during Mr. Scott's contempt hearing, admitted at least some of the allegations in the motion to withdraw.

Unfortunately, not all reverse benchslaps are similarly strategic. For example, Texas criminal defense attorney Adam "Bulletproof" Resposa (he's subsequently changed his state Bar site moniker to "Coach Reposa") made a vulgar gesture in court and was sentenced to 90 days in jail by Judge Jan Breland.[154] And then there is Jack Thompson who, having received his fair share of benchslaps, regularly expresses his poor opinion of the court in various and entertaining ways. Among Mr. Thompon's finest pleadings, meant to remedy "the court's inability to comprehend his arguments," is his motion entitled "A picture book for adults."[155]

It's clear that Mr. Thompson was past caring about the court's opinion when he filed his picture book. The same cannot be said for Arizona attorney Tajudeen O. Oladiran, whose anger at Judge Susan R. Bolton appeared to stem from caring too much. He set forth his feelings in his "Motion for a [sic] Honest and Honorable Court System," submitted to "the Dishonorable Susan R. Bolton."

This motion is filed by Plaintiffs' counsel, Tajudeen O. Oladiran, Esq. ("Mr. Oladiran" or "Taj"), pursuant to the law of, what goes around comes around. Judge Bolton, I just read your Order and I am very disappointed in the fact that a brainless coward like you is a federal judge.

I accused Suntrust Bank of racketeering etc, and many good lawyers in town told me the bank's executives would never be deposed, and that the case would go nowhere. I stupidly stuck to the notion that everyone is equal under the law etc. Boy was I wrong. The bank cancelled depositions set by the court, cancelled a hearing set by the court, and walked away without as much as a scratch.

My thanks go out to Larry Folks and Kathleen Weber who both warned me that I would lose (I should have listened to them). I apologize to all my clients. I know, I'm sorry does not repair the mess I made but, that's all I've got. To my family, words can't express my apologies; please remember me kindly.

Finally, to Susan Bolton, we shall meet again you know where. ☺

SUBMITTED this First day of October, 2009.

OLADIRAN LAW, PC
Attorney At Law
By /s/ Tajudeen O. Oladiran, Esq.[156]

Although this author is always pleased to see smiley emoticons in legal papers, the final sentences of Mr. Oladiran's pleading sound ominous. Legal blog Above the Law described the ultimate sentence as containing "the most menacing smiley emoticon ever."[157] Mr. Oladiran, who subsequently referred to the above motion as the "Whistleblower Pleading," proceeded to file lawsuits against four federal judges. His benchslap included a threat of disbarment, an order to show cause and a six-month suspension from federal practice. He's received subsequent discipline from the Arizona bar for similar conduct.[158]

Like many lawyers profiled in this book, Mr. Oladiran is an accomplished attorney. He graduated with honors from the Arizona State University College of Law before working for two major AmLaw100 law firms. He was actively involved in the state Bar and was only the second African-American lawyer elected to the Arizona State Bar Board of Governors in over 76 years. Shortly after filing his "Whistleblower Pleading," Mr. Oladiran ran unsuccessfully for Arizona Attorney General.[159]

Mr. Oladiaran's story demonstrates how good and well-meaning attorneys can be terribly affected by judicial conduct. It's possible he will never recover from whatever it is that pushed him over the edge in Judge Bolton's courtroom. When drafting their opinions and speaking with counsel, judges should remember that their words can have a lasting and potentially irrevocable impact that may extend far beyond what they intend. It makes one question whether benchslaps or judicial incivility are ever appropriate, even if seemingly warranted.

CHAPTER 10: Reflections

Although the earliest recorded benchslap dates to the 16th century, it is only in the past decade that the legal blogosphere has transformed bookish judges into benchslapping celebrities. Today, the modern American benchslap and the notoriety it fosters is part of the legal landscape that all practitioners must navigate. This final chapter considers the reasons for the recent rise in benchslaps and to what extent the phenomenon is for good or ill.

The Rise of Benchslaps

There are a number of reasons benchslaps have increased in recent years. Courts, frustrated with legal incompetence and increasing workloads, and with little way of managing either, turned to benchslaps in the late 1990s to manage courtroom conduct. Modern judges are under incredible pressure to manage a growing caseload of increasing complexity and with limited resources. In 1997, approximately 270,000 civil cases and 50,000 criminal cases were filed in the 94 federal district courts.[160] By 2010, there were more than 300,000 civil cases pending and 77,000 criminal cases.[161] During this same period, the number of active district court judges declined and resources for district courts dwindled even as cases, especially those involving detailed or voluminous discovery, became more complicated and time-intensive. In California, the state court budget has been reduced by hundreds of millions of dollars over the past three years. This April 17, 2012 news release from the Los Angeles Superior Court is typical of those being issued across the country:

> The Los Angeles Superior Court today announces plans for the most significant reduction of services in its history. By June 30, 2012, the Court will reduce its staff by nearly 350 workers, close 56 courtrooms, reduce its use of court reporters and eliminate the Informal Juvenile Traffic Courts.

> According to Presiding Judge Lee Smalley Edmon, "Staffing reductions due to budget cuts over the past 10 years have forced our court to reduce staffing by 24%, while case filings continue to increase. This has created incredible pressures on our court to keep up with our work. We cannot endure these pressures for much longer."

> In the current year, additional staffing reductions are required to deal with the fact that the state's budget crisis has resulted in a reduction to the California judicial branch of $652 million. The Court has managed its share of these cuts by spending down year-end fund balances, freezing wages,

furloughing court staff, and eliminating staff positions, achieving $70 million in ongoing savings as of last fiscal year.

"This year, the state cuts are forcing us to reduce our spending by an additional $30 million – on top of the $70 million in reductions we have already made," notes Edmon. "There will be as many as 350 dedicated, skilled court workers who will no longer be serving the residents of Los Angeles County. When we lose those people, we will no longer be able to shield the core work of the court – the courtroom – from the budget crisis."[162]

Even as courts experience dramatic reductions in judicial resources, they must respond to a decline in the quality of legal appearances. In the past decade, the number of annual graduates from U.S. law schools has increased nearly 20-percent. Many of these junior attorneys come from law schools where the quality of students and legal education has been much maligned. The American Bar Association, which accredits new law schools, has been either unwilling or unable to stem the tide of new law schools and law school graduates. As a result, judges may feel they need to address attorney competence head-on.

Judges may feel particularly inclined to benchslap incompetent attorneys when their performance is more than just an inconvenience to the Court. An adversarial legal system relies on advocates of relatively equal skill and resources. While a courtroom battle between skilled advocates yields a fair presentation of the evidence, a battle between unequal or unskilled attorneys can be a farce. As a juror in the Rakofsky trial noted, "Whatever momentary empathy any of us on the jury may have felt for [the attorney's] absolute ineptitude, we were quickly absolved by our knowledge that a young man's entire life was at stake." To the extent benchslaps can clear courtrooms of incompetent counsel, judges may be acting to save the very system of American justice.

And in the digital age, benchslaps foster change like never before. Just fifteen years ago, a staggering benchslap in a regional state court would never see the light of day. Today, that same opinion is circulated within hours and read by tens of thousands of attorneys throughout the country. Any judge with an axe to grind can reach a global audience by penning an opinion that is witty or scathing. For example, several pages of this book are devoted to the jurisprudence of the incorrigible Judge Sparks, whose opinions use humor (and occasional ridicule) to teach lessons about reasonableness, civility and collegiality. Celebrity aside, there is an incentive for Judge Sparks to use humor: the funnier his opinion, the more likely its message will affect aspiring, junior or incompetent attorneys. That may be good for the legal profession.

There's also a cultural explanation for the rise of benchslaps in America. During the past decade, judges often find themselves at the epicenter of the "culture wars," refereeing courtroom battles over controversial issues such as abortion, education, marriage equality and religious freedom. These cases are political dynamite. Regardless of their rulings, judges are accused of bias or incompetence. A written opinion offers jurists a rare opportunity to engage the public and respond to critics. For example, in *Schultz v. Medina Valley Independent School District*, Chief Judge Frank Biery concluded his opinion approving a mediated settlement with a moving "Personal Statement":[163]

A PERSONAL STATEMENT

During the course of this litigation, many have played a part:

To the United States Marshal Service and local police who have provided heightened security: Thank you.

To those Christians who have venomously and vomitously cursed the Court family and threatened bodily harm and assassination: In His name, I forgive you.

To those who have prayed for my death: Your prayers will someday be answered, as inevitably trumps probability.

To those in the executive and legislative branches of government who have demagogued this case for their own political goals: You should be ashamed of yourselves.

To the lawyers who have advocated professionally and respectfully for their clients' respective positions: Bless you.

SIGNED this ___9___ day of February, 2012.

FRED BIERY
CHIEF UNITED STATES DISTRICT JUDGE

Benchslaps and the Dignity of the Court _____

It is easy to appreciate why judges deliver benchslaps. But in many cases, opinions that rage against incivility or incompetence risk becoming examples of the very conduct they criticize. Indeed, benchslaps that cross the line between humor and ridicule undermine the seriousness and credibility of the judiciary. Judge Sam Sparks, discussed above, may have crossed that line when he issued the following opinion.

BE IT REMEMBERED on this day the Court reviewed the files in the above-styled causes, and now enters the following opinion and orders.

Non-parties Lance Langford, Erik Hoover, and Brigham Oil & Gas, L.P. invite the Court to quash subpoenas issued to them on behalf of Jonathan L. Woods, in relation to a matter currently pending in the United States District Court for the Western District of Louisiana, Lafayette-Opelousas Division, because the subpoenas were not properly served, are overly broad and unduly burdensome, and seek privileged information. In response, the Court issues the following invitation of its own:

Greetings and Salutations!

You are invited to a kindergarten party on THURSDAY, SEPTEMBER 1, 2011, at 10:00 a.m. in Courtroom 2 of the United State Courthouse, 200 W. Eighth Street, Austin, Texas.

The Party will feature many exciting and informative lessons, including:

- How to telephone and communicate with a lawyer;
- How to enter into reasonable agreements about deposition dates;
- How to limit depositions to reasonable subject matter;
- Why it is neither cute nor clever to attempt to quash a subpoena for technical failures of service when notice is reasonably given; and

- An advanced seminar on not wasting the time of a busy federal judge and his staff because you are unable to practice law at the level of a first year law student.

Invitation to this exclusive event is not RSVP. Please remember to bring a sack lunch! The United States Marshals have beds available if necessary, so you may wish to bring a toothbrush in case the party runs late.

Accordingly,

IT IS ORDERED that defense counsel Jonathan L. Woods, and movants' attorney Travis Barton, shall appear in Courtroom 2 of the Unisted States Courthouse, 200 W. Eighth Street, Austin, Texas, on THURSDAY, SEPTEMBER 1, 2011, at 10:00 a.m., for a memorable and exciting event …[164]

Judge Sparks, USDC,
Southern District of Texas

Judge Sparks' opinion spawned a frenzy of commentary in the legal blogosphere. This author received the opinion from five different outlets within a 24-hour period. And just a few days after the opinion was issued, Chief Judge Edith Jones of the Fifth Circuit issued a benchslap of her own – to Judge Sparks.

Dear Sam,

It has not escaped my attention, or that of my colleagues or, I am told, nationally known blog sites that you have issued several 'cute' orders in the past few weeks. The order attached below is the most recent.

Frankly, this kind of rhetoric is not funny. In fact, it is so caustic, demeaning, and gratuitous that it casts more disrespect on the judiciary than on the now-besmirched reputation of the counsel. It suggests either that the judge is simply indulging himself at the expense of counsel or that he is fighting with counsel in what, as Judge Gee used to say, is surely not a fair contest. It suggests bias against counsel.

No doubt, none of us has been consistently above reproach in our professional communications with counsel. We are all prone to human error. But no judge who writes an order should allow such rhetoric to overcome common sense.

Ultimately, this kind of excess, as I noted, reflects badly on all of us. I urge you to think before you write.

Sincerely,
Edith Jones.[165]

Judge Jones' e-mail was intended to be private. But as often happens in the digital age, the e-mail found its way into the hands of legal reporters and went viral. And while this author disagrees with Judge Jones' opinion that the order "was not funny," her e-mail does raise a host of issues relating to the role of benchslaps in modern jurisprudence.

Judge Jones' letter suggests that while a certain degree of humor or causticity may be appropriate, judges who rely in "excess" on such language may find themselves on a slippery slope. As in the case of former Judge Kent, who was described by colleagues and litigants as a "tyrant" and "giant," unchecked judges who begin using well-meaning barbs may, as their career develops, turn into benchslapping terrors.

This slippery slope is made more treacherous in the digital age. Benchslaps, particularly extravagant benchslaps like Judge Sparks', exhibit a certain degree of self-gratification. Obscure local judges who deliver monumental smack downs can find themselves headlining prominent legal publications (or even profiled in popular legal books). In the case of elected judges, such press can create a useful national profile of being "tough" or "no-nonsense." This kind of attention can be flattering and addictive, but Judge Jones rightly questions whether such notoriety for an impartial judge is appropriate.

As attorney Adam Cohen noted in *Time*, "[t]here is clearly an audience for this sort of mean-judge shtick. Judge Judy regularly beats Oprah in the Nielsen ratings, and last year she hauled in a reported $45 million ... still, judicial bullies may thrive on television, but they have no place in real courts of law."[166] As David Lat puts it, "[t]hese are judicial orders, not blog posts (where snark and entertainment are welcome)."[167] University of Baltimore law professor Garrett Epps leveled a similar criticism against Judge Posner, arguing that federal judges should treat "serious issues seriously."[168] Professor Epps encouraged the Seventh Circuit to issue a new opinion "written in a truly judicial voice."[169]

Aside from their indignity, benchslaps may undermine justice in more substantive ways. The credibility of an adversarial justice system depends upon zealous advocates, impartial judges and the public's confidence in both. Benchslaps, particularly those that cast aspersion on one party or the other, "suggest the judge's decision is being driven by personal animus rather than detached judgment."[170] This personalization of the judicial process undercuts the credibility of judges and the judicial system.[171]

One must also question whether derisive benchslaps belie poor judicial reasoning or effort. Are judges using ridicule to shirk their responsibility to resolve difficult disputes? Blogger Michael Williams of TheViewFromLL2 frames the issue this way:

> There are well-defined standards that apply to sanctions and other punishments for lawyers. Sometimes these standards are not especially easy to meet. I get the impression that sometimes judges use heated rhetoric to inflict the punishment of public shaming while not having to meet the standards that would apply to more traditional sanctions. Frankly, that approach is both lazy (as it avoids the work of imposing the sanction) and dishonest (as it avoids the rightful standard). If a lawyer's conduct in a case is appropriately condemned, the judge should impose an appropriate sanction – without nasty language – that will send that message. The rhetoric is probably best left to the politicians.[172]

The concern raised by Mr. Williams is a serious one because, unlike traditional sanctions, public shamings are not subject to judicial review. Even more disturbing is that a benchslap cannot be rescinded once it enters the legal blogosphere. This is true even if the benchslap is later found to be unjustified. Consider the Qualcomm Six, who received a benchslap of almost unparalleled severity from Magistrate Judge Major accompanied by hefty sanctions. Although the sanctions were lifted on appeal and Judge Major reversed her finding that the attorneys acted in bad faith, the humiliating opinion ended the big firm careers of at least four of the Qualcomm Six (and saddled them with a moniker that will follow them the rest of their lives). The severity and permanence of public shaming in the digital age is why attorneys like Joseph Rakofsky will go to foolish lengths to eradicate their cases from the Internet. Because of the damning effect of judicial take downs in the modern age, judges should exercise extreme restraint when issuing benchslaps.[viii]

Attorneys' Right to Free Speech _____

There are clear dangers associated with benchslaps. Although they can be a force for good, they are also a symptom of judicial tyranny that can threaten the very core of the American justice system. One way to offset this threat is for attorneys to speak out against judges who abuse their bully pulpit by issuing unwarranted benchslaps.

[viii] In *In re Spickelmier*, Slip Copy, 2012 WL 1190295, *f.14 (Bkrtcy. D. Nev., April 9, 2012), the court noted in a footnote that it would delay publication of its benchslapping opinion until after the time period for the filing of an appeal, thereby ensuring the affected attorneys would not be publicly shamed until after they had an opportunity to challenge the court's findings.

Of course, an attorney's free speech right to issue reverse benchslaps presents thorny problems of its own. Unlike the general public, attorneys operate as citizens *and* officers of the court. They have an obligation to respect and uphold the justice system both in and out the courtroom. As a result, many well-meaning attorneys who criticize judges and courts in their personal Bar.

In comments to Salt Lake City's *City Weekly*, attorney Charles Schultz criticized Utah's rural courts. "To use the term 'justice' for these courts is a joke," he said. "These are revenue courts." Schultz also accused Utah Judge Kevin Christensen of "routinely fail[ing] to advise [defendants] of their rights. It's a complete power trip for him."[173] Mr. Schultz's claims about Judge Christensen were supported by the American Civil Liberties Union who, in conjunction with the University of Utah Civil Rights Clinic, submitted an official complaint to the Utah Supreme Court regarding Judge Christensen's conduct.[174]

The Bench and the Utah Bar did not take kindly to Mr. Schultz's comments. He was disciplined for conduct "prejudicial to the administration of justice,"[175] and the Utah State Bar proposed an amendment to the state's Rules of Professional Conduct to prohibit an attorney from "knowingly making a false statement about the judicial system."[176] The amendment was designed to "[e]ncourage lawyers to defend the judicial system,"[177] and could have meant discipline for any Utah lawyer who failed to support or defend the justice system.

Despite the disciplinary action against him, Mr. Schultz was unrepentant. In an e-mail published in *City Weekly*, he made the following plea in support of attorneys' right to speak freely about the justice system.

The proposed addition RPC 08.02 ... prohibit[ing] knowingly making a false statement about the judicial system and requiring lawyers to defend the judicial system, should not be adopted. It is unconstitutionally vague and ambiguous, at best. Who determines when a statement about the judicial system is "knowingly false?" Who is to say that whatever person, committee, panel, or other entity that decides a statement about the judicial system is false, much less "knowingly false," is more qualified to determine if the statement is false or "knowingly false" than the person making the statement?

When I became a lawyer, I never dreamed that it meant giving up my Constitutional right to free speech under the First Amendment to the Constitution of the United States. However, it is very apparent that in Utah, lawyers are a subclass of citizens who have no rights under the First Amendment to the Constitution of the United States.

What is next? Will lawyers be required to kneel before entering court buildings? Will CLE mandate that lawyers take a class on how wonderful, marvelous, and perfect the judicial system is? Will a lawyer's letterhead be required to contain a reference stating how lucky he or she is to be permitted to be associated with such a wonderful and marvelous institution as the judicial system? Before they are permitted to enter a court building, will lawyers be required to kneel, and give thanks for being permitted to associate with such a holy and venerated institution as the judicial system?

Will lawyers be required to call judges "Your Worship, Your Holiness, Your Majesty," or some other reverent term?

I also hope the proposed Rule does not include "revenue courts." Although I know it does, and in fact, the motivation of this proposed rule is in response to the various articles written about what a joke and mockery of the legal system "revenue courts" are.

I shall never say anything good about "revenue courts!" I will accept any punishment rather than say anything good about "revenue courts!" In fact I will be disbarred before I will say anything good about "revenue courts!"

It is a very sad commentary on the state of the legal system in Utah when the powers that be feel the need to adopt a rule requiring lawyers to lie about the legal system. Well, at least the proposed change does not use the phrase "Justice System." That would truly be an oxymoron.[178]

Mr. Schultz is not alone in receiving discipline for his out-of-court comments. Florida defense lawyer Sean Conway was disciplined for blogging that Judge Cheryl Aleman was an "Evil, Unfair Witch."[179] (It's worth noting that Judge Aleman was herself subsequently reprimanded for demonstrating an "arrogant, discourteous and impatient manner" with counsel.)[180] Illinois attorney Kristine Peshek was disciplined for assigning to a jurist the moniker "Judge Clueless," and William Anderson, a lawyer practicing in Southern California, was suspended for out-of-court claims that his presiding judge showed favoritism and conspired with opposing counsel.[181] California attorney Stephen

Corris went one step further and referred to the entire San Bernardino County judiciary as a "cesspool of injustice" and suggested that local judges may be "in bed" with prosecutors.[182]

While some of these comments may go too far, there's clearly a balance to be struck between free speech and an attorney's obligation as an officer of the court. And it's been well established that the First Amendment does not protect comments that push the bounds of civility. As Judge William J. O'Neil of the Arizona Supreme Court once noted, attorneys "may not hide behind [their] First Amendment rights to ignore [their] sworn responsibilities."[183] Blogger Mauricio Hernandez described this tension in his blog, The Irreverent Lawyer, in this way:

> When it comes to what lawyers think of judges, lawyers must exercise the greatest degree of care and concern. Our ethical rules require us to accord the respect due to courts of justice and to judicial officers.
>
> There's a simple but important reason for this, it's to preserve the rule of law. To create and safeguard the public's confidence in the integrity of its judiciary, lawyers consent to restricting their First Amendment Free Speech rights in favor of supporting the state's interest in maintaining the public's trust in its legal institutions and processes.
>
> But here's the rub. Lawyers, especially those who regularly appear in court, have an *inside-baseball* view of the judicial process, that is, they have an insider's knowledge of the intricate details and occurrences not well known to outsiders…

Because lawyers are uniquely qualified by their experiences in court, they owe a higher duty to share that knowledge with the public, especially when it implicates a matter of public concern. Consequently, that's the tension that arises here.

How do we weigh the benefits to be gained by lawyers divulging matters of public concern against the risk of diluting if not damaging the equally important interest in upholding judicial integrity?[184]

Although it is difficult to determine the appropriate balance between these competing concerns, one way to check the judiciary's bully pulpit is to better define attorneys' right to free speech across all jurisdictions. In the abstract of her article *A Free Speech Right to Impugn Judicial Integrity in Court Proceedings*, Associate Professor Margaret Tarkington of the Indiana University Robert H. McKinney School of Law argues that

[A] free speech right to impugn judicial integrity must be recognized for attorneys – even, and perhaps especially, when acting as officers of the court and making statements in court proceedings. Such a right is necessary to protect the constitutional and other rights of litigants to an unbiased and competent judiciary. Further, the recognition of such a right in the attorney preserves litigants' access to courts and due process rights. These rights belonging to litigants are all but lost where attorneys are punished for or chilled from asserting them in court proceedings. … [T]he judiciary does not need to punish attorney speech impugning judicial integrity in order to protect its legitimate interests in the just adjudication of cases. In fact, by curbing speech in the presentation of claims, the judiciary undermines its own role and responsibility in remedying constitutional violations and providing fair proceedings.[185]

Of course, it's possible that embracing an attorney's right "to impugn judicial integrity" would simply degrade the dialogue between attorneys and jurists beyond its already alarming condition. This may be why, to the extent the Bench and Bar are concerned with attorneys' free speech, it is being limited rather than expanded. For example, South Carolina is among a number of states where courts and commissions are disciplining attorneys based solely on incivility, and Florida is the most recent of many jurisdictions to incorporate a duty of civility into its oath of admission.[186] Because of the difficulties inherent in defining the limits of attorneys' right to free speech, this author proposes a simpler antidote to the potential poison of benchslaps: benchpraise.

Benchpraise

Benchslaps hurt. They are embarrassing. They can undermine the American justice system. They can cause irreparable harm to attorneys' lives and careers, stifle free speech and impact judicial elections. And yet benchslaps are an increasingly utilized judicial tool to manage courtroom conduct and improve attorney's performance. Regardless of the balance of costs and benefits, it appears benchslaps are here to stay.

If benchslaps cannot be moderated, perhaps they can be offset or complimented by a technique familiar to parents across the globe: positive reinforcement. Judge Peggy Leen once famously described herself as a "school marm scolding little boys."[187] Her analogy is not unique. But among most parents, corporeal discipline is being replaced by positive reinforcement as an effective tool to improve children's behavior. While "benchpraise" may not have the ring of "benchslap," it could alter the dynamic and dialogue between attorney and judge in a productive way. And as the following opinion from Kentucky Judge Martin Sheehan proves, benchpraise can be every bit as funny.

The herein matter having been scheduled for a trial by jury commencing July 13, 2011, and numerous pre-trial motions having yet to be decided and remaining under submission;

And the parties having informed the Court that the herein matter has been settled amicably [Footnote 1: The Court used the word "amicably" loosely] and that there is no need for a Court ruling on the remaining motions and also that there is no need for a trial;

And such news of an amicable settlement having made this Court happier than a tick on a fat dog because it is otherwise busier than a one legged cat in a sand box and, quite frankly, would have rather jumped naked off of a twelve foot step ladder into a five gallon bucket of porcupines than have presided over a two week trial of the herein dispute, a trial which, no doubt, would have made the jury more confused than a hungry baby in a topless bar and made the parties and their attorneys madder than mosquitoes in a mannequin factory ...

1. The jury trial scheduled herein for July 13, 2011 is hereby CANCELED. ...

2. The Clerk shall engage the services of a structural engineer to ascertain if the return of this file to the Clerk's office will exceed the maximum structural load of the floors of said officer.[188]

Judge Martin J. Sheehan,
Kenton Circuit Judge, Kentucky

This author hopes judges will begin setting aside as much space in published opinions to praise attorneys who excel as they do benchslapping attorneys who fail. Unfortunately, that day may be far away. In the meantime, for those attorneys who are recipients of future benchslaps, learn from your experience and hope that any failure is simply a milestone on the road to success. And for those attorneys who are still laughing, please also feel a twinge of pity. If there's one thing you should have learned from this book it's this: you could be next.

Chapter 1 _____

[1] Oxford English Dictionary, Third Edition (Online Version) (March 2012), available at http://www.oed.com/view/Entry/252022?rskey=koscNV&result=2&isAdvanced=false#eid (last visited June 18, 2012)

[2] TMZ Staff, *Badass Judge Tackles Suspect – In Court!!!*, TMZ.com (March 24, 2009), available at http://www.tmz.com/2009/03/24/badass-judge-tackles-suspect-in-court/ (last visited June 18, 2012)

[3] Elie Mystal, *Judge of the Day: For Real*, Above the Law (March 25, 2009), available at http://abovethelaw.com/2009/03/judge-of-the-day-for-real/#more-11208 (last visited June 18, 2012);

Karen Sosa, *Judge of the Day: Stephen Belden*, Above the Law (September 4, 2009), available at http://abovethelaw.com/2009/09/judge-of-the-day-stephen-belden/#more-1433 (last visited June 18, 2012);

Matt Lait, *Man Curses Judge and His Lawyer Before Getting 50-Year Term in Death of Couple*, Los Angeles Times (August 20, 1991), available at http://articles.latimes.com/1991-08-20/local/me-1393_1_death-penalty (last visited June 18, 2012);

Associated Press, *Judge Orders Man's Mouth Shut with Duct Tape*, KVAL.com (April 21, 2009), available at http://www.kval.com/news/local/43357512.html (last visited June 18, 2012)

[4] John Bratt, *You Got Benchslapped!*, Baltimore Injury Lawyer Blog (March 18, 2011), available at http://www.baltimoreinjurylawyerblog.com/2011/03/you_got_benchslapped_1.html (last visited June 18, 2012)

[5] Count Christoph von Stoph-Stopherson, Urban Dictionary, def. *benchslap*, (October 18, 2001), available at

http://www.urbandictionary.com/define.php?term=benchslap (last visited June 18, 2012)

[6] Twitter, @BryanAGarner, November 29, 2012

Chapter 2 _____

[8] The State Bar of California, *California Attorney Guidelines of Civility and Professionalism*, Sections 4 ("Communications") and 11 ("Conduct in Court") (2007), available at http://www.saccourt.ca.gov/local-rules/docs/guidelines-civility-professionalism.pdf (last visited June 18, 2012)

[9] *Chamberlain Group v. Lear Corp*, 756 F.Supp.2d 938 (2010)

[10] *Klein-Becker, LLC, et al. v. William Stanley, et al.*, Case No. 05-cv-3449, Order on Motions in Limine (March 22, 2011)

[11] *Keystone Media International, LLC v. David B. Hancock*, , S.D. Tex., Order (April 23, 2007)

[11] *Avista Management, Inc. v. Wausau Underwriters Ins. Co.*, Case No. 6:05-cv-1430-Orl-31JGG , M.D. Fla, Order (June 6, 2006)

[13] *See, e.g.*, U.S. Department of Justice, Bureau of Justice Statistics, *Civil Rights Complaints in U.S. District Courts*, 1990-2006 (August 2008)

[14] *Jayhawk Capital Management, LLC, et al. v. LSB Industries*, Case No. 08-2561-EFM, Dist. Kan., Order on Motion to Continue (April 12, 2011)

[15] *Hyperphrase Technologies LLC v Microsoft Corp.*, WL 21920046 (W.D. Wis., July 1, 2003)

[16] *Masztal v. City of Miami*, 971 So.2d 803 (2007)

[17] *Id.*

[18] *Medtronic Navigation, Inc., et al. v. BrainLAB Medizinische Computersystems GMBH, et al.*, No. 98-cv-01072-RPM, Dist. Colo., Order for Award of Attorney Fees and Costs to BrainLAB Defendants (February 12, 2008)

Chapter 3 _____

[19] *Labor Force, Inc. v. Jacintoport Corp. et al.*, Case No. G-01-058 , S.D. Tex., Order Denying Defendant's Motion to Dismiss or Transfer Venue and Ordering Substitution of Counsel-Of-Record (June 7, 2001)

[20] *Republic of Bolivia v. Philip Morris Companies, Inc., et al.*, Case No. G-99-110, S.D. Tex., Order of Transfer (March 1, 1999)

[21] *Smith v. Colonial Penn Life Insurance*, Case No. G-96-503, S.D. Tex., Order Denying Motion to Transfer (Nov. 6, 1996)

[22] Brenda Sapino Jeffreys, Former Federal Judge Sentenced to 33 Months in Prison, Law.com (May 12, 2009), available at http://www.law.com/jsp/article.jsp?id=1202430621450&slret urn=1 (last visited July 12, 2012)

[23] Richard Connelly, *Federal Judge Sam Kent Gets Less Than Three Years in Prison*, Houston Press (blog) (May 11, 2009), available at http://blogs.houstonpress.com/hairballs/2009/05/federal_ju dge_sam_kent_gets_le.php (last visited June 18, 2012)

[24] Associated Press, *Kent Sentenced to Almost 3 Years in Prison*, Galveston Daily News (May 12, 2009), available at http://galvestondailynews.com/story.lasso?ewcd=d96de41f92 01daa4 (last visited June 18, 2012)

[25] *Id.*

[26] Chris Paschenko, *Former Judge Kent Moved to Florida Prison*, The Daily News (November 7, 2009), available at

http://galvestondailynews.com/story/146798 (last visited July 12, 2012)

27 *Smoot v. Mazda Motors of America, Inc.*, 469 F.3d 675 (2006)

28 Ted Frank, Smoot v. Mazda, PointofLaw.com: Information and Opinion on the U.S. Litigation System (November 29, 2006), available at http://www.pointoflaw.com/archives/003256.php (last visited July 12, 2012)

29 *Bradshaw v. Unity Marine Corporation, Inc.*, 147 F.Supp.2d 668 (2001)

30 *Thul v. Onewest Bank, FBS*, Case No. 12 C 6380, N.D. Ill., Memorandum Opinion and Order (January 3, 2013)

31 Skadden Arps attorney profile page, available online at http://www.skadden.com/professionals/john-h-beisner (last visited January 18, 2013)

32 Elie Mystal, *McCain Veep Vetter Culvahouse Tries to Hang On* (September 4, 2008), Above the Law, available at http://abovethelaw.com/2008/09/mccain-veep-vetter-culvahouse-tries-to-hang-on/ (last visited January 18, 2013)

33 *Thul v. Onewest Bank, FBS*, Case No. 12 C 6380, N.D. Ill., Counsel's Response to the Court's Order to Show Cause (January 10, 2013)

34 *Thul v. Onewest Bank, FBS*, Case No. 12 C 6380, N.D. Ill., Memorandum and Order (January 18, 2013)

35 M. Fleischer, *Judging Another Judge: A Case of the Nasties*, New York Observer (March 22, 1999), available at http://www.observer.com/1999/03/judging-another-judge-a-case-of-the-nasties (last visited June 18, 2012)

36 David Rosenzweig, *Injunction Prohibits Use of Stun Belts to Control Defendants*, Los Angeles Times (January 27, 1999), available at

http://articles.latimes.com/1999/jan/27/local/me-2074 (last visited June 18, 2012)

[37] Matt Lait, *Man Curses Judge and His Lawyer Before Getting 50-Year Term in Death of Couple*, Los Angeles Times (August 20, 1991), available at http://articles.latimes.com/1991-08-20/local/me-1393_1_death-penalty (last visited June 18, 2012)

Associated Press, *Judge Orders Man's Mouth Shut with Duct Tape*, KVAL.com (April 21, 2009), available at http://www.kval.com/news/local/43357512.html (last visited June 18, 2012)

[38] *Securities and Exchange Comission v. Mangan, et al.*, Case No. 3:06-cv-531, Transcript of Proceedings (October 24, 2007)

[39] Peter Lattman, *Law Blog Footnote of the Day: the Scooter Libby Trial*, The Wall Street Journal Law Blog (June 11, 2007), available at http://blogs.wsj.com/law/2007/06/11/law-blog-footnote-of-the-day-the-scooter-libby-trial/ (last visited June 18, 2012)

[40] *U.S. v. Libby*, Crim. Case No. 05-394 (RBW), Dist. D.C., Order (June 8, 2007)

[41] *In re Therese Cesar Garza*, Case No. 6180720, Illinois Attorney Registration and Disciplinary Commission, Complaint (April 25, 2012)

[42] David Lat, *Benchslap of the Day: Special Ed for DC ... Lawyers?*, Above the Law (November 1, 2007), available at http://abovethelaw.com/2007/11/benchslap-of-the-day-special-ed-for-dc-lawyers/ (last visited June 18, 2012)

[43] *Thompson v. The Florida Bar*, Case No. 07-21256-CIV-JORDAN, S.D. Fla., Order to Show Cause (September 24, 2007)

[44] *Thompson v. The Florida Bar*, Case No. 07-21256-CIV-JORDAN, S.D. Fla., Plaintiff's Verified Motion to Vacate Order to Show Cause (September 26, 2007)

[45] *Thompson v. The Florida Bar*, Case No. 07-21256-CIV-JORDAN, S.D. Fla., Order of Instructions to Pro Se Litigant (October 1, 2007)

[46] Alana Robert, *Anti-Porn Crusader May Face Sanctions for 'Meritless Filings'*, Daily Business Review (February 2, 2008);

Mike Fahey, *Jack Thompson Disbarred*, Kotaku (Gawker Media) (September 25, 2008, available at http://kotaku.com/5054772/jack-thompson-disbarred (last visited June 18, 2012);

Daniel Ostrovsky, *Fla. Bar Seeks Sanctions Against Morality Watchdog Jack Thompson*, Daily Business Review (February 8, 2008) available at http://www.law.com/jsp/article.jsp?id=1170928966137 (last visited June 18, 2012);

Alana Robert, *Sanctions Hearing Set for Lawyer Found to Have Humiliated Litigants, Other Attorneys*, Law.com, (May 5, 2008) available at http://www.law.com/jsp/article.jsp?id=1202421556225&slret urn=1 (last visited June 18, 2012)

[47] *The Florida Bar v. Thompson*, Case Nos. sc07-80 and sc07-354, Florida Supreme Court, Respondent's Verified Motion to Vacate This Court's Two Orders on the Basis of Florida Bar's Fraud (March 2007)

[48] *The Florida Bar v. Thompson*, Case Nos. sc07-80 and sc07-354, Florida Supreme Court, Report of Referee (July 8, 2008), available online at http://www.scribd.com/doc/2233184/Jack-Thompsons-childrens-picture-book-for-adults-Legal-Filing (last visited June 18, 2012)

[49] Staff, *One Year Ago Today*, GamePolitics.com (September 25, 2009), available at

http://www.gamepolitics.com/2009/09/25/one-year-ago-today (last visited June 18, 2012)

50 *Wolff v. U.S.*, Case No. 06-cv-00321-PB, Order (September 18, 2007)

Chapter 4 _____

51 *See, e.g.*, U.S. Department of Justice, Bureau of Justice Statistics, *Civil Rights Complaints in U.S. District Courts*, 1990-2006 (August 2008)

52 *Mazzeo v. Gibbons, et al.*, Case 2:08-cv-01387-RLH-PAL, Dist. Nev., Order re Emergency Motion to Forbid Improper Objections (July 27, 2010)

53 *D.L., et al., v. District of Columbia*, Case No. 05-cv-1437 (RCL), Order (May 9, 2011)

54 *Qualcomm Inc., v. Broadcom Corp.*, Case No. 05-cv-01958-B-BLM, S.D. Cal., Order Granting In Part and Denying In Part Defendant's Motion for Sanctions and Sanctioning Qualcomm, Incorporated and Individual Lawyers (January 7, 2008)

55 Kashmir Hill, *An Interview with One of the Qualcomm Six, Adam Bier (Or: Horror Story from A Young Associate, Wrongfully Sanctioned and Job Hunting During the Great Recession)*, Above the Law (April 15, 2010), available at http://abovethelaw.com/2010/04/an-interview-with-one-of-the-qualcomm-six-adam-bier-or-horror-story-from-a-young-associate-wrongfully-sanctioned-and-job-hunting-during-the-great-recession/ (last visited June 18, 2012)

56 Debra Cassens Weiss, *After Sanctions Are Lifted Qualcomm Lawyers React*, ABA Journal (April 15, 2010), available at http://www.abajournal.com/news/article/after_sanctions_are_lifted_qualcomm_lawyers_react_this_can_happy_to_anybody/ (last visited June 18, 2012)

[57] Administrative Office of the United States Court, Office of Human Resources and Statistics Division, *Federal Judicial Caseload: Recent Trends* (undated), available at http://www.uscourts.gov/uscourts/Statistics/FederalJudicialC aseloadStatistics/2001/20015yr.pdf (last visited June 18, 2012)

[58] *See, e.g.*, U.S. Department of Justice, Bureau of Justice Statistics, *Civil Rights Complaints in U.S. District Courts*, 1990-2006 (August 2008)

[59] Maura Dolan and Victoria Kim, Budget Cuts to Worsen California Court Delays, Officials Say, Los Angeles Times (July 20, 2011), available at http://articles.latimes.com/2011/jul/20/local/la-me-0720-court-cuts-20110720 (last visited July 12, 2012)

[60] *Capital Records v. Thomas Rasset*, Case No. 6-cv-01497-MJD –LIB, Order (November 1, 2010)

[61] *Justice v. Town of Cicero, et al.*, 682 F.3d 662, 665 (7th Cir. June 5, 2012)

[62] United States Patent and Trademark Office, Registration Number 2791458, Registrant Snell & Wilmer L.L.P., available at http://tess2.uspto.gov/bin/showfield?f=doc&state=4003: bkk 4vs.2.1 (last visited July 12, 2012)

[63] Allison Maynard, *Sound Off* (comments), Clear the Bench Colorado (April 15, 2009) (comment posted May 20, 2009), available at http://www.clearthebenchcolorado.org/sound-off/ (last visited June 18, 2012)

[64] *In re Application for Water Rights of the Southwestern Water Conservation District*, Case No. 01-CW-54, District Court Water Division, Motion for Rule 6b2 Extension to Respond to Bill of Costs (March 4, 2007)

[65] David Lat, *Lawyer of the Day: Alison Maynard*, Above the Law (March 8, 2007), available at http://abovethelaw.com/2007/03/lawyer-of-the-day-alison-maynard/ (last visited June 18, 2012)

[66] Jay O'Keefe, *Some Thoughts from Justice Millette*, De Novo: A Virginia Appellate Law Blog (September 8, 2009), available at http://www.virginiaappellatelaw.com/2009/09/articles/appell ate-practice/some-thoughts-from-justice-millette/ (last visited June 18, 2012)

[67] *Id.*

[68] *Gordon v. Green*, 602 F.2d 743, 744-45 (5th Cir. 1979)

[69] Judith D. Fischer, *Bareheaded and Barefaced Counsel: Courts React to Unprofessionalism in Lawyers' Papers*, 31 Suffolk U. L. Rev. 1

[70] *Slater v. Gallman*, 38 N.Y. 2d 1, 4, 339 N.E.2d 863, 864 (1975)

[71] *Kushner v. Winterthur Swiss Ins. Co.*, 620 F.2d 404, 408 (3rd Cir. 1980)

[72] *N/S Corp. v. Liberty Mut. Ind. Co.*, Case No. 96-55641, 1997 WL 656358, at *1 (9th Cir., Oct. 23, 1997)

[72] *Belli v. Hedden Enterprises, Inc.*, Case No. 8:12-cv-1001-T-23MAP, M.D. Fla., Order (August 7, 2012)

Chapter 6 _____

[74] *City of Mission Viejo v. Saddleback Valley Unified School District*, Case No. 30-2009-00300610-CU-WM-CXC, Orange County Sup. Ct., Minute Order (September 23, 2010)

[75] *Sanches v. Carrolton-Farmers Branch Independent School Dist.*, 647 F.3d 156, 172 f. 13 (5th Cir., 2011)

[76] *Henderson v. State*, 445 So. 2d 1364 (1984)

[77] *Nault v. Evangelical Lutheran*, Case No. 09-cv-01229-GAP-GJK, M.D. Fla, Order (September 15, 2009)

[78] Mr. Glasser's Florida bar attorney page, available at http://www.floridabar.org/names.nsf/0/397E837C0552A4C A85256A84001B1818?OpenDocument (last visited June 18, 2012)

[79] *In re Hawkins*, 502 N.W.2d 770, 770-71 (Minn. 1993)

[80] *David v. Village of Oak Lawn*, 1996 WL 494268, at *2 (N.D. Ill. Aug. 27, 1996)

[81] *Gardner v. Investors Diversified Capital, Inc.* 805 F.Supp. 874, 875 (D.Colo.,1992)

[82] *Trapp v. Schuyler Constr.*, 149 Cal. App. 3d 1140, 1141 (1983)

[83] *Ward v. Ward*, 88 N.C. App. 267, 269, 362 S.E.2d 847, 849 (1987)

[84] *Henderson v. State*, 445 So. 2d 1364, 1367 (Miss. 1984)

[85] *People v. Vasquez*, 137 Misc. 2d 71, 76, 520 N.Y.S.2d 99, 103 n.2 (1987)

[86] *P.M.F. Servs., Inc. v. Grady*, 681 F. Supp. 549, 551 n.1 (N.D. Ill. 1988)

[87] *State v. Bridget*, 1997 WL 25518 at *3 f. 3 (Ohio App. 8 Dist., 1997)

[88] *Duncan v. AT & T Communications, Inc.*, 668 F. Supp. 232, 234 (1987)

[89] Michael Sangiacomo, *Federal Court Dismisses Former Bratenahl Police Chief's Lawsuit*, The Plain Dealer (March 7, 2012), available at

http://blog.cleveland.com/metro/2012/03/federal_court_dis
misses_former.html (last visited June 18, 2012)

90 *Medical Dental Development LLC vs. Pierson Plt.,* Case No. 10-367447, Orange County Sup. Ct., Order Denying Motion for Summary Judgment (September 10, 2010)

91 Max Frumes, Jacquelyn Ryan and Eleanor Goldberg, *Judge Slams NU's Attorney as Subpoena Hearing is Delayed,* Medill Reports (November 10, 2009), available at http://news.medill.northwestern.edu/chicago/news.aspx?id=1 45743 (last visited June 18, 2012)

92 *United States v. Venable,* 666 F.3d 893 (4th Cir., 2012)

93 *Mobile Logistics LLC v. Old Dominion Freight Line,* Civil Action H-12-2297, S.D. Texas, Order (November 7, 2012)

94 *First Time Videos, LLC v. Does 1-46,* Civil Action H-11-4431, S.D. Texas, Order Striking Report (March 16, 2012)

95 *Armstrong v. Tygart,* Case No. A-12-CA-606-SS, W.D. Texas, Order (July 9, 2012)

96 *In re Shepperson,* 674 A.2d 1273 (1996)

97 *Espitia v. Fouche,* 314 Wis.2d 507 (Wis. App., 2008)

98 *Rodriguez v. Chen,* No. 1996 WL 159810, at *7 (D. Ariz. Feb. 7, 1996)

99 *In re Shepperson,* 674 A.2d 1273 (Vt. 1996)

100 *Cook v. Hilltown Township,* 1990 WL 109985, at *2 (E.D. Pa. Aug. 1, 1990)

101 Jonathan Turley, *Decoupling the Staple Story: New York Jurists Changes Account Over Negligent Stapling Story,* Res Ipsa Loquitor (blog) (October 2, 2009), available at

http://jonathanturley.org/2009/10/02/new-york-jurist-challenges-account-over-negligent-stapling-story/ (last visited June 18, 2012)

[102] Martha Neil, *Negligent Stapling of Filing Cited by Judge in Tort Action*, ABA Journal (September 24, 2009) available at http://www.abajournal.com/news/article/negligent_stapling_of_filing_helps_persuade_judge_to_toss_tort_action/ (last visited January 18, 2013)

[103] *Stanard v. Nygren*, 658 F.3d 792 (7th Cir., 2011)

[104] *Peck v. Martin*, Case No. 1131-cv-04225, Cir. Ct. Greene County Miss., Motion to Make More Definite and Certain (April 23, 2011)

[105] *Id.*

[106] Kathryn Wall, *Attorney Has Harsh Words for Bluebaum*, News-Leader.com (June 15, 2011), available at http://www.news-leader.com/article/20110615/NEWS01/106150392/Attorney-has-harsh-words-Bluebaum (last visited June 18, 2012)

[107] Kathryn Wall, *Attorney Bluebaum Responds to Accusations About Her 'Poor Usage of the English Language'*, News-Leader.com (June 28, 2011), available at http://www.news-leader.com/article/20110628/NEWS01/106280352/Attorney-Bluebaum-responds-accusations-about-her-poor-usage-English-language- (last visited June 18, 2012)

[108] *Peck v. Martin*, Case No. 1131-cv-04225, Cir. Ct. Greene County Miss., Docket

[109] *Peck v. Martin*, Case No. 1131-cv-04225, Cir. Ct. Greene County Miss., Notice of Dismissal (November 8, 2011)

[110] *In re Shepperson,* 674 A.2d 1273 (Vt. 1996)

[111] *In re Hogan,* 112 Ill. 2d 20, 23-4, 490 N.E.2d 1280 (1986)

[112] *Lee, et al. v. Cook County, et al.,* 635 F.3d 969 (7th Cir., 2011)

[113] http://michaeljgreco.com/

[114] *Id.*

[115] Martha Neil, *Blistering 7th Circuit Opinion Fines Lawyer $5K, Orders Him to Alert Clients to Possible Malpractice,* ABA Journal (March 23, 2011), available at http://www.abajournal.com/news/article/blistering_7th_circuit_opinion_fines_lawyer_5k_orders_him_to_alert_clients_/ (last visited June 18, 2012)

[116] *Hartz v. Administrators of the Tulane Educational Fund, et al.,* 2008 WL 1766886, at *8 (5th Cir., 2008)

[117] Alan Childress, *Never Saw This Argument to the Fifth Circuit Before: 'I Try Not to Read That Many Cases, Your Honor'* (comments), Legal Professions Blog (April 17, 2008), available at http://lawprofessors.typepad.com/legal_profession/2008/04/i-have-never-se.html#comments (last visited June 18, 2012)

[118] *Id.*

[119] *Id.*

[120] Jeff Gameso, *Even the Judge Couldn't Take It,* Gameso – For the Defense (April 2, 2011), available at http://gamso-forthedefense.blogspot.com/2011/04/even-judge-couldnt-take-it.html (last visited June 18, 2012)

[121] *District of Columbia v. Deaner,* Case No. 2008 CF1 030325, Mistrial Declared (Docket) (April 1, 2011)

[122] Keith L. Alexander, *D.C. Superior Court Judge Declares Mistrial Over Attorney's Competence in Murder Case*, The Washington Post (April 1, 2011), available at http://www.washingtonpost.com/local/dc-superior-court-judge-declares-mistrial-over-attorneys-competence-in-murder-case/2011/04/01/AFlymrJC_story.html (last visited June 18, 2012)

[123] Rend Smith, *N.J. Lawyer Doesn't Care What D.C. Thinks of Him*, Washington City Paper (April 4, 2011), available at http://www.washingtoncitypaper.com/blogs/citydesk/2011/04/04/n-j-lawyer-doesnt-care-what-d-c-thinks-of-him/ (last visited June 18, 2012)

[124] *Rakofsky et al. v. The Washington Post el al.*, Index No. 105573/11, Order to Show Cause, p. 8-9 (January 3, 2012)

[125] *Rakofsky et al. v. The Washington Post el al.*, Index No. 105573/11, Complaint (May 11, 2011)

[126] Scott Greenfield, *Rakofsky v. Internet, Part Deux (A Juror Verdict)*, Simple Justice (May 13, 2011), available at http://blog.simplejustice.us/2011/05/13/rakofsky-v-internet-part-deux-jury-talk.aspx (last visited June 18, 2012)

[127] Rend Smith, *N.J. Lawyer Doesn't Care What D.C. Thinks of Him*, Washington City Paper (April 4, 2011), available at http://www.washingtoncitypaper.com/blogs/citydesk/2011/04/04/n-j-lawyer-doesnt-care-what-d-c-thinks-of-him/ (last visited June 18, 2012)

[128] Eric Turkewitz, *Joseph Rakofsky – I Have an Answer for You*, New York Personal Injury Law Blog (May 26, 2011), available at http://www.newyorkpersonalinjuryattorneyblog.com/2011/05/joseph-rakofsky-i-have-an-answer-for-you.html (last visited June 18, 2012)

[129] Scott Greenfield, *Rakofsky v. Internet, Part Deux (A Juror Verdict)*, Simple Justice (May 13, 2011), available at http://blog.simplejustice.us/2011/05/13/rakofsky-v-internet-part-deux-jury-talk.aspx (last visited June 18, 2012)

[130] AngelAnalyzes, Urban Dictionary, def. *Rakofsky Effect*, (June 29, 2011), available at http://www.urbandictionary.com/define.php?term=rakofsky+effect (last visited July 12, 2012)

[131] Jamison Koehler, Joseph Rakofsky's Former Client Sentenced to 10 Years, Koehler Law Blog (May 4, 2012), available at http://koehlerlaw.net/2012/05/joseph-rakofskys-former-client-sentenced-to-10-years/ (last visited July 12, 2012)

[132] *Rosario v. Ercole*, 601 F.3d 118 (2nd Cir. 2010)

[133] *Wilson v. Wainwright*, 474 So.2d 1162, 1164 (Fla.,1985)

[134] *In re Spickelmier*, Slip Copy, 2012 WL 1190295 (Bkrtcy. D. Nev., April 9, 2012)

Chapter 8 _____

[135] *Id.*

[136] Search Results for "Jonathan Lee Riches," Above the Law, available at http://abovethelaw.com/?s=jonathan+lee+riches (last visited July 11, 2012)

[137] *The Florida Bar v. Thompson*, Case Nos. sc07-80 and sc07-354, Florida Supreme Court, Report of Referee (July 8, 2008), available online at http://www.scribd.com/doc/2233184/Jack-Thompsons-childrens-picture-book-for-adults-Legal-Filing (last visited June 18, 2012)

[138] *In re Riches*, 2008 WL 3978059 (S.D. Ga., August 26, 2008)

[139] *Riches v. Dierks*, 2008 WL 714069 at *7 (N.D. W.Va., March 14, 2008)

[140] *Washington v. Alaimo*, 934 F. Supp. 1395 ((S.D.Ga. 1996)

[141] *Washington v. Alaimo*, cv695-104, S.D. Georgia, Motion to Apologize (March 25, 2011)

[142] *Washington v. Alaimo*, Case No. cv695-104, S.D. Georgia, Order Denying Motion to Apologize (March 29, 2011)

[143] *Schlessinger v. Salimes*, 100 F.3d 519, 523 (Seventh Cir. 1996),

[144] John Grant, *Andrew Shaw Hopes to Become First Asian-American Milwaukee Mayer*, The UWM Post (February 18, 2008), available online at http://www.uwmpost.com/2008/02/18/andrew-shaw-hopes-to-become-first-asian-american-milwaukee-mayor/ (last visited June 18, 2012)

[145] *Trustees of Columbia University v. Jacobsen*, 53 N.J.Super. 574 (1959)

Chapter 9

[146] *Gonzalez-Servin v. Ford*, 662 F.3d 931 (7th Cir., 2011)

[147] Joe Palazzolo, *Who's the Ostrich?*, The Wall Street Journal Law Blog (November 28, 2011), available at http://blogs.wsj.com/law/2011/11/28/whos-the-ostrich/ (last visited June 18, 2012)

[148] *U.S. v. Black*, 530 F.3d 596 (7th Cir., 2008)

[149] *Goldberg v. Mount Sinai Medical Center of Greater Miami, Inc.*, Case No. 07-1210-BKC-LMI, S.D. Fla., Order to Show Cause Why William P. Smith, Esq. Should Not Be Suspended From Practice Before Thei Court Including Revocation of His Current Pro Hac Vice Status (May 21, 2007)

[150] Staff, *Justice Overturns Lawyer's Sentence for Insulting Judge, The New York Times* (October 21, 1999), available at http://www.nytimes.com/1999/10/21/nyregion/justice-overturns-lawyer-s-sentence-for-insulting-judge.html (last visited June 18, 2012)

[151] *Id.*

[152] *Idaho v. John Thomas Lorimer*, Case No. CR-MD-2011-0002954, District of Ada County, Motion to Withdraw (August 12, 2011)

[153] Mauricio Hernandez, *Turnabout is Fair Play? Ballsy Lawyer S Laims Juris by 'Oy Vey,' Expect Consequences,* The Irreverent Lawyer (September 10, 2011), available at http://lawmrh.wordpress.com/2011/09/10/turnabout-is-fair-play-ballsy-lawyer-slams-jurist-but-oy-vey-expect-consequences/ (last visited June 18, 2012)

[154] Jan Breland, *Lawyer Reposa, Who Made Lewd Gesture in Court, Gets Probation from State Bar,* Austin Statesman (May 5, 2010), available at http://www.statesman.com/blogs/content/shared-gen/blogs/austin/courts/entries/lawyer_discipline/ (last visited June 18, 2012); see also Reposa state bar attorney profile, available on line at http://www.texasbar.com/AM/Template.cfm?Section=Advanced_Search&template=/Customsource/MemberDirectory/MemberDirectoryDetail.cfm&ContactID=236231 (last visited June 18, 2012)

[155] *The Florida Bar v. Thompson*, Case Nos. sc07-80 and sc07-354, Florida Supreme Court, Report of Referee (July 8, 2008), available online at http://www.scribd.com/doc/2233184/Jack-Thompsons-childrens-picture-book-for-adults-Legal-Filing (last visited June 18, 2012)

[156] *Oladiran v. Suntrust Mortgage, Inc., et al.*, Case No. 2:09-CV-01471-SRB, Dist. Az., Plaintiffs' Counsel's Motion for a Honest and Honorable Court System (October 1, 2009)

[157] Kashmir Hill, *Taj Oladiran's 'Motion of the Year' Earns Him Sanctions*, Above the Law (October 11, 2010), available at http://abovethelaw.com/2010/10/taj-oladirans-motion-of-the-year-earns-him-sanctions/ (last visited June 18, 2012)

[158] *In re Tajudeen O. Oladiran*, Case No. MC-10-0025-PHX-DGC, D. Ariz., Order (September 21, 2010)

In the Matter of a Member of the State Bar of Arizona, Tajudeen O. Oladiran, Case No. SB-11-0057-D, Sup. Ct. Ariz., Judgment and Order (August 8, 2011)

[159] Kashmir Hill, *Taj Lives! (And He's Pissed)*, Above the Law (October 27, 2009), available at http://abovethelaw.com/2009/10/taj-lives-and-hes-pissed/ (last visited June 18, 2012)

Chapter 10 _____

[160] Administrative Office of the United States Court, Office of Human Resources and Statistics Division, *Federal Judicial Caseload: Recent Trends* (approx.. August 2002), available at http://www.uscourts.gov/uscourts/Statistics/FederalJudicialCaseloadStatistics/2001/20015yr.pdf (last visited June 18, 2012)

[161] *See, e.g.*, U.S. Department of Justice, Bureau of Justice Statistics, *Civil Rights Complaints in U.S. District Courts*, 1990-2006 (August 2008)

[162] Los Angeles Superior Court Public Information Office, *News Release: Los Angeles Superior Court's Presiding Judge Announces Courtroom Closures* (April 17, 2012), available at http://www.lasuperiorcourt.org/courtnews/Uploads/1420124

1713575312NRCOURTCLOSUREPLAN4-17-12.htm (last visited June 18, 2012)

163 *Schultz, et al. v. Medina Valley Independent School District*, Case No. SA-11-CA-422-FB, W.D. Tex., Opinion and Order of the Court Concerning Joint Motion to Approve Settlement and Enter Consent Decree (February 9, 2012)

164 *Morris v. Coker, et al.*, Case Nos. A-11-MC-712-SS, A-11-MC-713-SS, A-11-MC-714-SS, A-11-MC-715-SS, W.D. Texas, Order (August 26, 2011)

165 John Council, *Chief Judge Takes U.S. District Judge Sparks to Task in an Email*, Texas Lawyer (September 12, 2011) available at http://www.law.com/jsp/tx/PubArticleTX.jsp?id=1202514158040&slreturn=1 (last visited June 18, 2012)

166 Adam Cohen, *A Real Life Judge Judy Gets Smacked Down*, Time U.S. (August 18, 2010), available at http://www.time.com/time/nation/article/0,8599,2011494,00.html (last visited June 18, 2012)

167 David Lat, *Benchslap of the Day: Judge Sparks Burns More Attorneys*, Above the Law (August 29, 2011) available at http://abovethelaw.com/2011/08/benchslap-of-the-day-judge-sparks-burns-more-attorneys/ (last visited June 18, 2012)

168 Debra Cassens Weiss, *Slapdash Posner Needs to be Reined In by 7th Circuit, Says Las Prof*, ABA Journal (January 16, 2013), available at http://www.abajournal.com/news/article/law_prof_7th_circuit_needs_to_rein_in_slapdash_posner/?utm_source=maestro&utm_medium=email&utm_campaign=weekly_email (last checked January 18, 2013)

169 *Id.*

170 Michael Williams, *Are "Benchslaps" Really Appropriate*, TheViewFromLL2, (September 13, 2011), available at

http://viewfromll2.com/2011/09/13/are-benchslaps-really-appropriate/ (last visited June 18, 2012)

171 *See, e.g.*, Reynold Holding, *Judges Can Be Tough Without Getting Personal,* Slate (May 9, 2012), available at http://www.slate.com/blogs/breakingviews/2012/05/09/leo _strine_rips_into_martin_marietta_when_are_judges_too_catt y_.html (last visited June 18, 2012)

172 *Id.*

173 Eric S. Peterson, *Box Elder County's Broken Court,* City Weekly (April 20, 2010) available at http://www.cityweekly.net/utah/article-10839-box-elder-countys-broken-court.html (last visited June 18, 2012)

174 *Id.*

175 Eric S. Peterson, *Censored by the Bar,* City Weekly (June 9, 2010) available at http://www.cityweekly.net/utah/blog-3725-censored-by-the-bar.html (last visited June 18, 2012)

176 Utah RPC 08.02, available at http://webster.utahbar.org/news/2010/04/notice_of_propos ed_amendments_25.html (last visited June 18, 2012)

177 *Id.*

178 Eric S. Peterson, *Censored by the Bar,* City Weekly (June 9, 2010) available at http://www.cityweekly.net/utah/blog-3725-censored-by-the-bar.html (last visited June 18, 2012)

179 John Schwartz, *A Legal Battle for Lawyers: Online Attitudes vs. Rules of the Bar,* New York Times (September 12, 2009) available online at http://www.nytimes.com/2009/09/13/us/13lawyers.html (last visited June 18, 2012)

180 *Id.*

[181] Cal. Bar Journal Staff, *Nasty Comments About Judges May Still Invite Discipline*, Cal Bar Journal (April 1998), available online at http://archive.calbar.ca.gov/calbar/2cbj/98apr/98apr-22.htm (last visited June 18, 2012)

[182] *Id.*

[183] *In re Ziman*, Case No.s 10-1394, 10-2329, 11-0130, Report and Order Imposing Sanctions (April 30, 2012)

[184] Mauricio Hernandez, *Lawyers Can't Say Unkind Things About Judges*, The Irreverent Lawyer (September 18, 2009), available at http://lawmrh.wordpress.com/2009/09/18/lawyers-cant-say-unkind-things-about-judges/ (last visited June 18, 2012)

[185] Margaret Tarkington, *A Free Speech Right to Impugn Judicial Integrity in Court Proceedings*, Boston C. L. Rev., Vol. 51, p. 363 (2010)

[186] G.M. Filisko, *You're Out of Order! Dealing with the Costs of Incivility in the Legal Profession*, ABA Journal (January 1, 2013), available at http://www.abajournal.com/magazine/article/youre_out_of_ order_dealing_with_the_costs_of_incivility_in_the_legal (last visited January 18, 2013)

[187] *Mazzeo v. Gibbons, et al.*, Case 2:08-cv-01387-RLH-PAL, Dist. Nev., Order re Emergency Motion to Forbid Improper Objections (July 27, 2010)

[188] *Kissel v. Schwartz & Maines & Ruby Co., LLC, et al.*, Case No. 09-CI-00165, Kenton Cir. Ct., Kentucky, Order (July 19, 2011)

About the Author

Matthew A. Bowers is a travel writer, web designer, graphic artist, science fiction aficionado, slow-pitch softball pitcher and Little League coach. He's also an active attorney with an unhealthy interest in benchslaps. A refugee from the demands of life at a large law firm, Matthew now practices labor and employment law at a Los Angeles based labor union. He lives in Burbank, California with his wife and three children.

Please send press and other inquiries to
info@travelsseries.com.

www.ingramcontent.com/pod-product-compliance
Lightning Source LLC
Chambersburg PA
CBHW051447170526
45166CB00001B/151